JOURNEY TO JOY

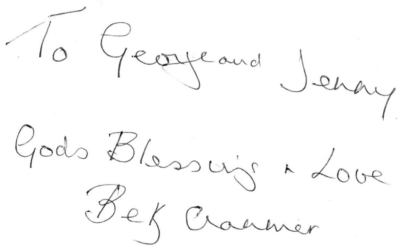

To George and Jenny

Gods Blessings & Love
Bety Cranmer

A Memoir By Betty Cranmer

Written and Edited with Cynthia Karnoscak Wigdahl
Cover Design by Patricia Cranmer

ISBN: 1463525117
ISBN-13: 9781463525118
LCCN: 2011908823
CreateSpace, North Charleston, South Carolina

ACKNOWLEDGEMENTS

In every way this project was a labor of love, and
those who lent their support to it were extremely generous.
To each we wish to express our immense gratitude:

To Betty's brother, Bill, and his wife, June, for a lovely afternoon
sharing their warm hospitality, while reminiscing through
Bill's World War II photo albums;

To Betty's daughter-in-law, Patricia, for so readily and lovingly lending
her artistic talents to the cover design and over seeing the digital
preparation of some of the photographs;

To those who read the manuscript with open hearts and keen editorial eyes —
Betty's son, Holbrook, Cyndi's husband, Jim,
and her friend and fellow writer, Eileen; and

To the many other family members and friends who offered valuable
conceptual input, as well as, devoted hours of prayer.

THANK YOU!
Betty and Cyndi

DEDICATION

This is written for the praise of the glory of God and
for the joy set before my precious children —
Susan, Holbrook, Allen, Bruce, Jeanie and Forrest;
my grandchildren — Leah, Michael, Emily, William,
Forrest, Ethan, Hannah and Nina; and
my great-grandchildren — Keller and Zea.

TABLE OF CONTENTS

FOREWORD

Why are people of all ages so captivated when they meet Betty Cranmer? That she speaks "the Queen's English" is always winning, especially to Americans, and she has an endearing smile and vibrant blue eyes that still dazzle as she approaches her 90th birthday. Beyond these qualities, I believe there is a genuine openness to all people—Betty truly welcomes anyone and everyone to share a moment of life with her and, if time and circumstance allows, perhaps even more.

Children and adults alike call her "Miss Betty." She has taught most of the younger generations in her Rocky Mountain, Colorado, community in some form or other since 1970. Today's students who read with Miss Betty in first grade are the children of those who read with her years ago. She would be hard-pressed to go anywhere in Grand County and not meet someone she knows—or at least someone who knows of her.

You could say Betty is somewhat legendary there. Nearly everyone knows the Cranmer name from the central "Cranmer" ski run at Winter Park Ski Resort. It was so named for her father-in-law, George Cranmer, a Denver politician and public works developer. Yet, her presence in the county reaches far beyond that notoriety. It is and always has been on a very personal level that Betty has invested herself in children and families and community life.

In 2007, after years of devoted service to elementary-aged children in the East Grand School District, Betty received a fitting honor as evidence of her generous spirit. She was nominated by then superintendent of schools, Robb Rankin, to receive the prestigious CASEY Award, which is given annually by the Colorado Association of School Executives. Betty was honored by the organization as "the most outstanding non-educator" in the state.

Mr. Rankin related that whenever he would meet Betty at school or elsewhere, he would thank her for her generous contribution. In true form, Betty would quickly correct him—thanking him instead for allowing her to do what she dearly loves.

Betty does not pay attention to her celebrity and even now finds it somewhat disconcerting that a book should be written about her. She would rather talk about her children, grandchildren, and great-grandchildren… and about the goodness of God, and the relationship she has enjoyed with Him for almost 50 years.

Still, Betty's life journey intrigues those who hear it because she has come to a place of freedom and joy as a survivor of World War II England, of multiple loss of loved ones, and of near devastation of her own life. She is most often asked to relate the stories from the early years, yet she is quick to describe the difference of living then as though God did not exist, and now, having experienced God as loving father and gentle healer and companion.

It is precisely Betty's humility and openness to God and life that makes her so irresistible. She resists telling anyone what they should do, choosing instead to quietly and fervently pray and entrust them to God's guidance and care.

She is quite simply about nurturing—people, especially children, and animals, particularly Black Labradors. She possesses a devotion and passion that has never diverted—becoming first a dutiful nurse, then a loving mother, later a caring schoolteacher and Sunday school instructor, and now a tireless volunteer. She even gently nurtures plants with a little conversation just for them—so it's no wonder she has a bountiful garden. The great thing is that Betty would think nothing of all this—it is simply the fabric of her life and breath all wrapped up in a joyful package.

When you meet Betty, you cannot mistake the pure joy that bubbles forth from her. This isn't just momentary happiness or circumstantial laughter. It's pure, enduring, magnetic JOY. The first time I met Betty, she was bubbling over with it, and it was infectious.

In the fall of 2002, I walked into a gathering of women in our small rural town, and Betty was there. As the program got going, she was asked to relate to the group a particularly courageous tale about a ski adventure she experienced with her son, Forrest, many years earlier. Listening to her, I knew immediately this was no ordinary woman. Other bits of her journey trickled into her sharing, and by the end of it, I was convinced I needed to know her.

That day, I invited myself into Betty's life. There was a prompting in my spirit, so I introduced myself with the awkward pronouncement: "I am a writer and I think your life story should be written." The seed of that prompting produced this book, and in my life, so much more. She graciously, and without hesitation, invited me for tea... and opened up her heart.

That was nearly nine years ago, and along the way this project has ebbed and flowed. It began with afternoon tea and homemade biscotti, sitting huddled near a roaring woodstove in her cozy home. It was often the high point of my week. At first, there were simple questions and hand-written notes. As we became more purposeful, I came with lists of probing questions and a tape recorder. Leaving these sessions, I realized a kindred relationship was growing from the seed of this project. Early on, I started calling Betty my joy mentor.

Knowing her as friend, mentor, sister, mother, I am convinced that Betty's intricate life tapestry is one woven by a loving and good and pursuing God. I have relived up-close the longings and the disappointments, the loving and the losing, the fight for life and the assurance of divine help and presence that shaped this great soul. For me, the experience has been thoroughly life giving, and has helped form my own journey toward joy. Being a part of Betty's life and helping to preserve her story in print has been a gift of God's great grace to me.

It would embarrass Betty for me to describe her as one incredible woman—but I'll take that risk. As you read on, I am confident you will discover that for yourself. My hope is simply that the journey shared within this cover—the living letters of Betty's life—will inspire and open your heart, as she has mine.

— Cyndi Wigdahl

INTRODUCTION

Where It All Began for Me

Being an English woman living in the United States and having come to this country right at the end of World War II, people I meet are rather curious about me. In many ways I consider my life to be pretty ordinary. Yet, when I think of the sweep of it all—as with other people's stories—it all seems quite extraordinary.

When I agreed with Cyndi to put the stories of my life in print I had no idea what a humbling experience it would be. She tells me I have a great memory. I hope that's true. We have worked hard on what appears in these pages—going over and over the details of each story. At each telling I thought, *"Well, there can't be anything more to say about that one"*—but somehow there always would be. I imagine there is yet more that could be said.

I hope with this writing to preserve for God's glory and for the encouragement of my beloved family the stories I have lived and the journey I have traveled. I have absolutely loved the remembering and the honoring of the memory of the people and the times of which we have written. All of it has shaped me and paved the way for true joy to be found—a joy I believe resides in the heart of God for each of us.

Of My Beginnings in England:

I was born into a working-class family just outside of London on August 29, 1921. I was the youngest of three children and the only girl; my brothers were Cyril, the oldest, who died in 2000, and Bill, now 91. My parents were Alfred Ernest Vernon Andrews (my father rather liked having three names because it was a very English thing) and Dorothy Eleanor Short. My given name was Betty Marguerite Andrews.

We lived closest to my mother's family—she was one of eight girls— and their family home was within walking distance of ours. It was within this family unit that I experienced warm and wonderful relationships as a child.

Many Saturdays were spent with Mother's family for afternoon tea. I would take my cousins out for walks—two in the perambulator or pram, as we called a baby carriage, and two alongside me. It was a glimpse of heaven for me because I always loved babies.

That love began when I was about the age of seven—I would go to my Aunt Nancy's to take her young son, Tony, out in the pram while she did her housework. I also got to be present at the births of a couple of my cousins. Particularly when Teddy was born, I remember the film *Showboat* first came out and my Aunt Violet loved to play the recording of the music. We did that over and over again while I was helping with the new baby—listening to and singing the song "Only Make Believe." Even now, when I hear that song, I can shut my eyes and go right back to their manor cottage in Littlehampton, Sussex.

On other Saturdays, my father would take me to Woolworth's department store to see if they had any English China bunnies for sale. It was very kind of him because he knew I loved them. Generally, my father was rather stern. In England at that time children were to be seen more than heard; discipline and respect were required of them more than warm feelings of love for their parents.

Although my father's sternness was hurtful to me as a young girl, now I see that he never had the opportunity for a loving relationship with his own father because he had died when my father was just 11 years old.

With the nature of my father's business in the film world, he was often absent from us as a family and he usually did not go on family holidays. The one trip I remember my father being with us was to the Channel Isles in the English Channel near the French coast of Normandy.

More often it was my mother and brothers and I who made short weekend trips. We would leave London for Sussex or Worthing. Some weekends we would go to the South Coast with my aunts and uncles and occasionally my father was able to join us. We would camp overnight and return on Sunday.

My father worked as general sales manager for Pathé Films, originally a French production company that diversified in the United Kingdom. During the war years the company mostly produced the popular newsreels, but they also made feature-length films. It was a well-known film company in the early days, but not one of the biggest.

I didn't go very often to church. My brothers went because they sang in the choir. Whenever I did go, which was to the Anglican Church of England, I wondered about God but he seemed very distant.

My brothers attended a private boys' school and I was sent to a private girls' school called Buehler House High School. It was not a high school in the American sense but more of an extension school for girls ages eight and older. I attended there until the age of 12.

Two sisters ran Buehler House. One of them would lead worship and prayer for the Catholic children in the school, and the other would lead worship and prayer for those of us in the Church of England. We always started school with prayer and hymn singing and we studied Scripture as a subject.

I was taken out of Buehler House because of an incident that happened when my parents once made a short trip to Scotland. On this occasion Bill and Cyril wanted to invite two neighborhood girls, Pat and Pam McFarland, over to the house. They were very nice looking girls—twins—and their father was a film star. All the neighborhood children considered them to be rather different because sometimes they put on make-up.

Pat and Pam came over and we ate baked beans on toast—a favorite English treat—and we played cards. It was just a nice time and then they went home.

However, the rendezvous did not go unnoticed thanks to a neighbor lady, Mrs. Williams. She saw the two girls leave our house and go down around the corner to their home. When my parents returned, Mrs. Williams told my mother she was quite surprised that they had allowed these girls to come to our house while they were away. Especially in those days in England, people's homes were quite private and you didn't just go over casually for a visit.

Of course, my parents confronted us. We denied it but our live-in maid, Molly, told on us. It was a Monday when my parents first returned and my father told us he would give us our punishment on Saturday. So we stewed about it all week.

Cyril had to give mother and father money out of his earnings from working at a furniture company. Bill had to stop participation in the Scouts for a while. But when it came to me, my punishment seemed the most severe; to this day I am not sure why except that my parents may have wanted to protect me from the potential influence of the twins. Their punishment was to take me out of Buehler House and send me away as a boarding student at a convent.

My mother and father and I went to visit this very old convent to have a tour of the facility and then to meet with the mother superior. When we went into the dormitory we saw the wooden beds lined up head-to-toe very close together. Then we saw the classrooms and the rest of the building. It was all very dark and dismal.

My parents knew it to be a good school, but by the time we sat down to talk with the mother superior, my father couldn't quite do it. The place seemed more like an orphanage than a boarding school.

Instead, they sent me to a technical day school for domestic science, which would be something like the home economics programs that used to be taught in American schools. I traveled alone each day on the bus. We studied the usual subjects—English, history, math—and then we also learned cooking and home management. For these subjects we actually worked in groups of three girls and were assigned to a house the school owned to be responsible to run it for a week. My team bought all the groceries and planned the meals, while other teams came to do the cleaning.

I enjoyed the program but it was not the sort of school where one would receive matriculation as we call it in England, or what would be equal to an American general education diploma (GED). Without matriculation I did not have the opportunity to go on to college. It was 1938, I was 18 years old, and my father simply wanted me to go to work.

My great love, my great solace all my growing up years had been children. I wanted to have a lot of them someday, and I dreamt about becoming one of the prestigious Norland nannies. The Norland Institute of England, now the Norland College, was a greatly respected two-year study program for young ladies. It produced nannies of the highest caliber to care for children of the old aristocracy, from infants up to six years of age. One of my aunts kept a Norland nanny, and she would tell me all about it—how they were given a flat in the house and how they took care of the nursery.

To become a Norland nanny remained my greatest aspiration all the way through school, but at the end my father said, "No." He did not want to pay for me to learn to care for other people's children; he thought I should simply wait to have children of my own.

So I took a job working for a trichologist, assisting with hair-replacement treatments. While I was working in London, I met my first young love Ted Oakley, an Australian. One evening I joined my brother Bill at a dance class because he needed a partner. Ted was there and I recall dancing quite a bit with him. By the end of class Bill consented when Ted asked if he could take me home. That was the beginning of our courtship.

Ted was training as a bomber pilot with the Royal Air Force in preparation for Australia's involvement in the war. He and I continued to date and, for a time, I continued my commute to London for my job.

The effects of war were being felt in more and more areas of our lives. Travel became difficult, blackouts became common practice, and food became more costly and scarce. Young people, too, began behaving differently, breaking with convention and marrying quickly.

Ted and I were about to be engaged when the war engulfed England. Soon he began running regular missions.

The last time I saw Ted, he was sending me off from Paddington Station to Redding. I remember the exact date—May 6, 1940—because I was leaving to help with the birth of my cousin, Jim.

With war going on in Europe and increasing threats that England would be swept up in the conflict, my mother and I moved to Sussex in 1939. We had a small three-acre plot of land there, about 30 miles out and about 30 miles from the South Coast. Half of it was wooded and on the other half was a cabin. Adjacent to our property was Furnace Farm and on the farm was a duplex—we lived on one side and a farmer lived on the other.

Shortly after we moved there some of our cousins came to live with us, so I needed to quit my job and stay in Sussex to help with the farm and to care for the children. I loved the area because I knew it well from our family visits when I was a child. Bill and I used to ride bikes on the country roads, and we rode horses at a nearby riding stable.

The farm was about five miles outside of East Grinstead. I helped to work the farm for a time, making hay. The horse would be on a lead pulling a big rake-like piece of equipment that I actually sat on. I would go through and pull the hay into big piles and then release it. Then the farmer and I would toss the hay piles into a cart. It was very hard work. On this particular farm it was just the farmer and I. I wasn't enrolled in the land army—I was doing that work just to help.

One day I went swimming in a nearby lake and was bitten by a horsefly. A few days later, I woke up and noticed the red line of blood poisoning going up my leg.

By the time I told my mother, I didn't feel well at all. The doctor came to the house right away but by the time he arrived, I was unconscious. The doctor said he couldn't move me because it might kill me, so they brought in a nurse who stayed with me around the clock. I don't remember much during those days. They put me on sulphanamide, which was used to fight infections before antibiotics were discovered. The doctor told my parents, "Forty-eight hours will tell us whether she will live or die."

When the critical timeframe passed, they moved me to the hospital in the hope of getting me to come out of the coma. Apparently, I was not fighting the coma—I did not seem to want to come out—and it lasted around seven days.

Just before I was bitten I had learned that Ted had gone out on a mission and was missing in action. He had been flying a bombing mission over the Maastricht Bridges in Holland. When he had first gone missing we thought he could have been taken as a prisoner of war. Then, several days later, his best friend reported that he was pretty sure Ted went down with the plane because he had seen him go in to bomb the bridges and he did not see him come out. I was brokenhearted.

Ted was my first love—a wonderful, wonderful man—and now he was gone. When I finally did wake up in the hospital, I only half remembered the ordeal of the horsefly bite and the blood poisoning. All I could think of was the aching disappointment of losing Ted. I saw my mother and father first and said, "Oh, I'm still alive—I wish I wasn't."

The war raged, with bombs falling all around us. Once I was out of the coma and dealing with my disappointed dreams, I felt I needed to do something. So I began volunteering at a small, private hospital in East Grinstead.

The many cases being handled there were severe—lots of soldiers who suffered terrible burns. They were asking for volunteers to help handle the caseload. I joined the Voluntary Aid Division (VAD). Once I learned more about the job we were to do, I remember saying to my mother, "I don't think I can do it—the smell of burnt flesh is so strong."

My mother told me to try it for a few weeks to see how it might work out, which I did. Still the desire to do more, to serve in a more significant way, drove me a step further, and I ended up joining the Women's Royal Air Force. I wanted to nurse possibly on a fighter station. Only basic training was required during the crisis, which consisted of marching, saluting, discipline and cleaning toilets. It was considered the fast track.

That was a tough stretch. We were sent to Morecambe in the north of England near Blackpool, which is near Liverpool, and we were living in billets. To be "billeted out" was to live in housing provided by civilians for military personnel. There were about five of us together, all women—wanting to serve as nurses. To our amazement, the lady who housed us gave us the same meal for two months. Every day it consisted of potatoes and tinned carrots and a long portion of tinned corned beef. We ate it, reminding each other with the encouragement, "Well, it's food."

From there I went for nurse's training, which was also a crash course. It wasn't the usual four-year program—it couldn't be. We had only a few months before we needed to report for duty. So, they crammed it in—we had to do all the anatomy and the whole thing in a very short time—very basic study in all the necessary medical subjects. We did it in six weeks in Nottingham.

I thought we would be taking temperatures and doing baths—not giving shots or anything more involved. When I finished my training, there was a great need for personnel to work in the burns and plastic surgery unit now set up at East Grinstead, Sussex. They saw in my record that I had already volunteered at that hospital so they sent me right back to the same place. I really did not want to go back, but the cases were desperate ones and they needed a lot of help.

The unit was called the Queen Victoria Cottage Hospital. There were still two regular wards for the local people but the rest of the facility was made into long wards, like Quonset huts, where the wounded soldiers were treated.

Two brine baths were set up off of Ward 3. That became the main burn unit.

This is where I did dressings and cleaning of burns all day long. It was difficult work to get used to—the smell was particularly awful—but I figured it was better than cleaning bedpans or making beds.

In England, the registered nurses were called sisters, perhaps from the "sisters of mercy." These were not Catholic nuns, just nurses. Our Air Force unit at the hospital was very small—a sergeant and about four men and me. The registered nurses did not like what we were assigned to do as nurse orderlies—perhaps they thought they should be doing our tasks because they had full training and we did not. Needless to say, working alongside them could get quite tense at times.

In wartime I served a total of four years—the first in the VAD and the rest in the Air Force—and all those years in the Queen Victoria Hospital in East Grinstead.

CHAPTER ONE

A War Too Close

I was so frightened I couldn't move—couldn't open my eyes. There were quick bursts of noise all around. It seemed as though the world was ending.

When I dared to peek, I found I was clinging to a lamppost. "*Where was Henry?*" I looked around and saw him a long way down the hill. He was all right.

When the chaos began, we had been walking down a quiet residential street away from the cinema at White Hall. I don't remember what was playing, but we had left the movie house early before the film ended. Henry had wanted to stay, but I needed to be back at the hospital by 4:30 p.m. sharp. It was payday and our sergeant always wanted us in uniform for a proper pay parade.

"I have to go," I told Henry.

"Let's stay and see the ending," he said. "You're just afraid of your sergeant."

"That's not it," I said. "I just have to go. If you want to stay you can find your own way back."

He relented.

I pushed Henry's wheelchair in the direction of the hospital. It was not like the ones we have today. It had four small wheels and a board that went out straight from the seat on which he could rest his legs.

I pushed him through the small town, past the main shops, on what we called the high street. East Grinstead was the main town for the outlying districts in Sussex—there were many shops and several churches.

This was market day and in the morning the town had been full of people. Now, as we walked toward the edge of town, there was nobody around. It was a clear day. We were about two miles from the hospital, and we were walking down a good hill with big trees at the bottom of it.

Suddenly, we spotted a bomber flying low over the trees ahead of us. It came so low and close to us that I could almost see the pilot in the cockpit, and as he went by I shouted, "That's a Gerry!" The German swastika was clearly visible on the side of the plane.

The pilot circled back, flying right over us, and opened fire. I suppose he thought he would just pick us off because we were both clearly in uniform.

There had been no sirens and no warning. The pilot must have come through our lines without being spotted. He was just one lone plane.

In the instance he fired on us I didn't think. I didn't respond as a nurse having to care for my patient no matter what. Impulsively, I grabbed the first thing at hand—the lamppost—and I held on with my eyes shut tight.

Henry rolled down the street and ended up several yards away at the bottom of the hill. When I looked for him, I was thankful he was upright. Later, he told me that was no small feat as he plummeted down the hill— somehow he managed to successfully grab and hold onto one of the wheels until he stopped.

In the spray of bullets, the pilot missed us completely. I don't know— perhaps he fired just to frighten us. Seeing we were in the clear, Henry and I quickly made our way back to the hospital—about a 20-30-minute journey.

Once inside we heard the news reports and learned that the pilot had dropped a bomb in town. I took Henry straight to his ward and quickly got gowned up to help with the casualties. Soon they started bringing them in to the hospital. There were so many of them and not enough room—so we laid them all over the floor.

Somebody told us that the cinema had been hit, but it wasn't until later that we learned the details. The German pilot had bombed the cinema right after he shot at us. Eighty people had been killed there and more than 250 were wounded. It was all quite shocking. They never even found the remains of the people sitting next to us at the movie that day.

I could hardly believe how close the war had come to us—too close.

The reality of it all was very hard for me. It being market day, I knew my two aunts and my mother had gone into town to do their weekly shopping. I was so worried, but there was no time to linger on that type of thinking. There were patients to be cared for—lots and lots of patients. I needed to focus on doing my duty as a nurse.

The ones they knew were dead were put in the nurses' recreation room, which was in a building off of the hospital. Some of those coming in were dying from shrapnel wounds. We were putting our fingers right on wounds to stop the bleeding, because we did not have enough tourniquets.

It was all so very hard. All the time I was working I was wondering if I might pull back the sheet from one of those being brought in and discover my mother or one of my aunts or cousins.

That day nearly all the doctors had gone to the neighboring town for meetings. There were only two doctors on duty. We worked through a lot of that afternoon and evening until all of the casualties were treated or received the needed surgeries.

Thankfully, by the end of the day, I learned none of my family was injured or killed in the attack. They had left town before the bomb fell.

Military service was now compulsory. Everyone from 18 to 40 years of age was required to serve—men and women. Working at the burns and plastic surgery hospital, I grew up quickly. One day I was a schoolgirl, the next I was serving my country in this great world conflict.

Back in East Grinstead after my training, I went again to live in a billet and was allowed to go home on the weekends. Being "billeted out" I had a small room, staying with a funny lady and her husband. It seemed to me she was almost six feet tall and her husband was shorter than I was. They had one child.

The burn center at Queen Victoria Cottage Hospital was a particularly difficult place to work because the cases were so terrible. It became one of the most famous burns and plastic surgery units in the country where a very famous plastic surgeon, A.H. (Archibald) McIndoe, was in charge. He was pioneering revolutionary work in the field and restoring life and dignity to men who were completely disfigured by their war injuries.

Not only military personnel were cared for there, but civilians as well. It was wonderful, groundbreaking work and that made it worthwhile. You felt as though you were truly helping these people.

The plastic surgeons at East Grinstead became world renowned for the advancements in rebuilding and restoring faces—noses, lips, chins, and ears—and much more. Because of the nature of the armament in World War II soldiers suffered badly from horrendous burns.

Surprisingly, it was in this challenging environment where I was to meet "Henry" as we knew him. Henry was a tall, handsome flight lieutenant from Denver—an American flying for the Royal Canadian Air Force. He was a graduate of Harvard University in engineering. Before the war, he worked for the Mountain States Telephone and Telegraph Company in Denver, Salt Lake City, and then Ogden, Utah.

But Henry was concerned that America was not going to get into World War II, so in 1940 he went to Calgary and joined up. He was deployed to England early in 1942, and served as an officer and a pilot going out regularly on flying missions.

In June 1942, while piloting a bomber over the North Sea near the Frisian Islands off the coast of Holland, his plane crashed. He spent 14 days in a dinghy trying to stay alive and hoping to be rescued. The cold and wet, plus lack of circulation, caused the eventual loss of his toes and part of one of his heels. One witness said his toes came right off when they first removed his boots.

Henry was close to death, but somehow miraculously lived. Just the night before he came to Queen Victoria Hospital, they had picked him up from the dinghy, which had been his lifeboat. He was brought to our hospital to have his feet cleaned up for grafting. At first he was just another patient.

At check-in the nurse in the admitting office asked him, "What is your name?" "Frederick Holbrook Mahn," he replied.

"Well," she retorted, "we can't call you that here. You look like Henry Fonda so we're going to call you 'Henry.'" And the name stuck.

Awkwardly for Henry, the first time he and I met, we were in one of the two bathrooms in our ward where the nurses cleaned up the patient's wounds.

Our daily job was to scrape the dead skin area around their particular injury and later to dress their wounds. This was standard procedure in preparation for plastic surgery and skin grafting.

For the severely burned patients this wasn't a painful process because the nerves were completely deadened. We used specially designed "McIndoe Forceps," with narrow pointed ends, to scrape the dead skin, and then we meticulously dressed the area.

In those days we didn't have penicillin so we used sulphanamide disinfectant powder and Vaseline gauze that we made and then put on quite tight. We would wrap wet saline dressings over the wound and then wrap a bandage over that. It was critical to keep the wound area clean and dressed, ready for surgery when the time came.

I encountered Henry when he was sitting in one of the bathtubs. I usually worked in the second bathroom but the regular nurse stationed in the first bathroom was absent that day, so I was sent in to clean up Henry's feet. It was not a pleasant job. For Henry the abrasions in his heel were to the bone.

That was my job and, quite honestly, I did not even think about who this new patient might be. As I walked into the bathroom I was fully gowned from head to toe—all that was showing was my eyes—so I guess I looked rather mysterious.

We did not speak to each other, but afterward I learned from the other orderlies, who were all male, that Henry had asked, "Who was that person who came in to clean up my feet—all I saw was her eyes?" They gave him my name. Then he asked, "Please, if it is at all possible, don't have her come in here again." Much later in our story I read a letter Henry had written to his parents where he told them he had fallen in love with me—with my eyes— that very first time he saw me.

An interesting twist to this story—shortly before Henry came to our hospital—I had gone home from work for lunch to see my mother. She began telling me about an amazing story she had heard on the wireless.

She said, "There was this young American who was telling a story about how he had been stranded in the North Sea for 14 days—he told of his survival experience."

"Oh, isn't that interesting?" I responded.

Then, a few days later, I was home again and said to my mother, "Well, that young officer on the radio is now at our hospital."

By the time Henry and I had contact again after that first day in the hospital, I knew who he was and what he had been through but nothing else about him. It was appealing to us over there that Henry was an American, and he was handsome and had a beautiful smile. He was an officer—a lieutenant— with two stripes, so he was a rather impressive man to me.

When I would walk by his bed, he began asking a little bit about me. Soon he started asking me to take him into the officer's recreation room at the hospital or to have a beer or something when I was off duty. When he was able to get out, I started taking him in his wheelchair into town to the local pub. These were common outings for many of the personnel with the patients who were rehabilitating. Mr. McIndoe believed it was good for the patients to get out and become normalized with their new condition among other people.

Eventually, I took Henry out every time he wanted to go—several times a week. Soon we spent all of our free time together. Sometimes I felt I was burning the candle at *three* ends—I would work a good shift, which under wartime conditions felt like two shifts, and then Henry and I would go out.

The work at the hospital was strenuous. We had to lift these men in and out of the baths and then bandage them. In addition, there was the emotional stress of the cutting off of fingers, ears and toes. It was traumatic for these patients. I had to become sort of tough dealing with all of that and the men's bad language. I learned to say, *"O fiddle!"* and *"O sugar!"* You had to make light of it when you could.

Still, the work was fascinating. The burns and plastic surgery unit was known for the pedicle grafts. Pedicles are stems or stalks of skin tissue that form connective bridges as the doctors take skin from the stomach and begin the process of grafting. First, they might attach it to the wrist for a few weeks and watch the health of it and the blood supply—the stomach is a very nice lump of good healthy tissue—then they might move it to the shoulder. Eventually a man would get a new nose from it, but it was a long process.

At Queen Victoria Hospital we had soldiers of all types—officers and privates, Americans, British, Canadians—they were all mixed in together and it kept everything equal. It was a good environment.

THE STORY OF
THE DINGHY

During the time we spent together, although Henry didn't like to talk much about the crash, I did learn more of the details of how he survived the days in the dinghy and how he was rescued in the North Sea.

There were four of them flying in a Bristol Blenheim bomber. It was believed they crashed due to engine trouble. One of them was killed in the crash and the three surviving took to the dinghy. When they looked for their food ration most of it had been contaminated because of the petrol. They only found one small canteen of water.

Both German and British planes flew over them—even American ones. Henry said there were several planes that came down quite close to them. On the eighth day, a German plane seemed to have spotted the dinghy because it circled overhead for 45 minutes, before being chased away by a British plane that did not notice the dinghy. No

cont.

The saline baths were used for a period of time with patients before grafting was attempted—the saline kept the skin tissue moist and supple. This benefit was discovered after pulling soldiers from the waters of the English Channel after the Battle of Dunkirk—their burn wounds healed much more easily. When I was first at the center as a VAD nurse we had only one bath with salt water pouring into the bath—a year later when I returned they had built two more baths onto that ward.

Henry had been in our hospital since his crash in June and by Christmas 1942, I knew we were getting serious with each other. I was working on Christmas Day listening to Bing Crosby sing "White Christmas" (that was the year the song first became popular). Sitting with Henry and holding his hand I thought, *"Yes, I am falling in love with this man."*

He was in our hospital for nearly 10 months. We were trying to save his feet with a "postage stamp" skin grafting procedure. These were little grafts actually the size of postage

28

stamps, being taken from the inner thigh and grafted onto the feet. But, the procedure didn't work for Henry.

After losing his toes, he also still had an area in the back of his heel that was not healing. The doctors tried to clean it up to graft it and considered doing what they called a "leg flap." For this, they would take his foot and put it to his calf, grafting them together until the skin took. Unfortunately, they could never get the foot clean enough to do the graft.

After trying these various treatments they decided they would have to amputate his legs below the knees. The initial loss of his toes was caused because of lack of circulation, with frostbite and Gangrene. The eventual amputation of both of his lower legs was necessary to keep the infection from spreading.

By May 1943, the hospital administration wanted to send Henry back to Canada for the rest of his treatment because he was a Canadian officer. Being the favorite "dark-eyed boy" at the hospital—thoroughly spoiled by the surgeon, the anesthesiologist and even Mrs. Dewar of the

British or American planes spotted them for two weeks.

As the days wore on, one of the airmen started drinking seawater and died. Henry and the other airman put him over the side. On the 10th day the other man did the same thing and Henry had to put him over.

There was nothing to do but lie in the boat, and he was pretty weak from lack of food and water. He was beginning to lose consciousness from time to time. Even though it was June, the North Sea was very cold—he was wet, cold, and had no feeling left in his feet at all.

Henry said on the 13th day a seagull landed on his chest and because it was alive and he hadn't seen anything alive for several days he just left it there for a while. Then he realized he would have to kill it and eat it, so he rang its neck and opened it up with a penknife. He drank the blood and ate the fish paste in its stomach.

After that he became semiconscious again, not remembering

cont.

much more until the 14th night when a motored gunboat of the British Navy came by on patrol for land mines. They switched off their engines and when they did Henry stood up and shouted to them. Once they spotted him and picked him up, he was taken to a hospital in Lincoln where they first took off his boots.

Dewar dynasty who would bring him whiskey—Henry's wing commander, Ross Tilley, got permission for him to stay in England.

When it came time to perform the amputations the doctors wanted to send him to Roehampton Hospital in London where they had been doing this type of procedure for years. Henry didn't want to go because he didn't want to be separated from me, so Mr. McIndoe made it possible for the orthopedic surgeon to come from London to East Grinstead.

He was put in a private ward, and they took off his legs below the knees. His room was in the main ward—not in the Air Force wards—and he was treated royally. The surgery was followed by a time of convalescing without his legs. Later, he did have to go to Roehampton to be fitted with prosthetic legs. He was there for about two weeks.

After that, his first objective was to learn to walk and his second objective was to get retrained in order to go back into action as a

Spitfire pilot. Those were the goals he set for himself, and shortly after that, we were engaged. He said to me, "I'm not going to marry you until I can walk."

In wartime, by necessity, weddings were very creative affairs. Young couples made do with very little. My dress was lovingly made by one of my dear aunts, a wonderful seamstress, who pieced it together from the lace of an old tablecloth. We had no coupons to buy clothing—civilians got coupons—but military personnel were provided only their uniforms.

We were married in East Grinstead at the little church of St. Swithin's— and it seemed nearly the entire town came to celebrate with us. We were married on Leap Day, February 29, 1944. Henry thought that was so wonderful because by his reasoning that meant he only had to remember our wedding anniversary every four years.

To me it was all a wonderful love story. Henry wooed me with his great smile and good looks and our love blossomed in the midst of that awful war.

CHAPTER TWO

Into My Darkest Days

Henry got his legs and in our early days of marriage we went up to Lincoln, in the North Country, where Henry went into training as a fighter pilot. He knew he could not fly bombers again because he would not be allowed to carry a crew. So he set his sights on flying Spitfires.

These small, one-person fighter planes really won the Battle of Britain. They were absolutely amazing. In the daylight during that battle you would see hundreds and hundreds of German bombers coming over—and then you would see these few little Spitfires flying around trying to shoot them down. Because of their size they were extremely maneuverable.

In the fall of 1944 I became pregnant again, having miscarried a first baby. The doctors had told me not to get pregnant for another year but it happened quickly after Henry returned from a trip to the U.S. I had gone up to London to meet him, and we stayed at the romantic Savoy Hotel. Because of the pregnancy, I was soon discharged from active duty.

Amazingly, just before our baby was due the war was suddenly over and Henry never went back into active duty. Life was about to change dramatically yet again.

Susan was born in June 1945, and we spent most of that summer down in East Grinstead where we rented a small room with a kitchen.

With the end of the war Henry began to think toward the future. Through the Royal Canadian Air Force he was offered a scholarship to Cambridge University. He knew he did not want to return to the United States to live. He had been back to Colorado once for about a month in March 1944, right after we were married, because his mother died suddenly. It was a very difficult loss for him because they had been very close.

Even though his father wanted him back in the U.S., by the time Henry returned to England from that trip, he knew it was not what he wanted. He was very different after his experience in the war and his amputation. He found it comforting to be where people accepted him more freely for who he was now.

By August 1945, we moved to Cambridge for Henry to pursue a master's degree in engineering. We found a small place and Henry enrolled at Trinity College. I took care of the baby and Henry went to school.

England, after World War II, represented a new start for Henry and he pursued that through his studies. I would say he was able to lead a fairly normal life after his rehabilitation. He could even pretty easily manage the three flights of stairs to our apartment. Yet, in some ways, he never fully recovered from his war injuries and the physical trauma of it all. We had no particular concerns about his health, and life went on until March 1946.

Henry woke up one night complaining of excruciating pains in his stomach. Amazingly, we had a doctor who lived next door to us. We were in a third-floor flat in a building with no elevator. I called the doctor at two o'clock in the morning and he came right over and examined Henry. He said we must get Henry quickly down the stairs and to the hospital. The doctor took him because I needed to stay with Susan as, in those days, babies were not allowed in hospital.

When I called the next morning to check on Henry, the doctors told me they had fought for his life all through the night. What they discovered was that his whole lower bowel had perforated. He had developed diverticulitis, a disease caused by infection in the intestines, and peritonitis, an infection in the abdomen often caused by abdominal trauma. The doctors were not at all sure that it was not something Henry may have had for quite awhile—he may have had a propensity for it, as his father would also later die from it.

Again, we didn't have penicillin in those days so after the doctors examined Henry and operated on him to determine what was wrong, they just stitched him up and said they could not do anything more.

Henry was conscious after the surgery, but I could not see him right away. It was a proper British hospital, not like our American hospitals today where you can go in almost any time of the day. There, visiting hours were strictly from two to four in the afternoon.

One of the toughest things I had to face was when Henry was desperately ill the third night after surgery. The hospital was short-staffed and they called and asked if I could help because they knew that I was a nurse. My mother had come to be with me to help care for the baby, so I could go back and forth to the hospital. She stayed with Susan and I went to help care for Henry.

We knew he was in the last stages of life. When I went in to stay with him, he was not actually in a coma—he could talk. But the staff told me not to give him anything by mouth at all. There was nothing in the room—no sink, no cups—no other patients. Nothing.

When I first walked in Henry said, "Please give me some water."

It broke my heart, but I had to say, "Henry, I can't."

He said, "I knew *you* would give me water."

It was so very frustrating—the hospital staff had no compassion—there was no bending the rules. All I could think about was all those days in the dinghy that Henry went without water and now here he lay dying.

Henry died that night, March 5, 1946.

I remember so plainly: It was the middle of the night when he died. They put me in a bed in the women's ward because I couldn't go home then. There was just a screen around it to give me some sense of privacy, because it was one of those wards with the women all lined up in beds in a row.

They gave me something pretty strong to help me sleep. When I woke up, I realized, *"Here I am… and Henry's gone."* I just started crying and I guess I was crying loud enough that a patient walking by heard me. She came over and said, "Oh dearie, don't cry—it's not all that bad being in hospital."

"No," I said, "I am a nurse, I don't mind being in hospital. My husband just died." She didn't know what to say to that, so she just shut the curtain and walked away.

In my heart, all these years later, I still remember deeply loving Henry.

The day before Henry died he had said to me, "You go to Dad. You go and he will take care of you financially."

We were pretty certain I was about two months pregnant and Henry wasn't at all sure what kind of pension he might get from the Canadian Air Force. We didn't have any savings.

Things in England were quite difficult after the war. There was still a lot of rationing. Some people felt those days were worse than the war years.

Henry's father called and began to work out the details to get Susan and me on a flight to the United States. Tickets were very difficult to acquire right after the war—many people were being evacuated to America and Canada and many of these were children and families. Still, he managed to get us flights on Pan Am Airlines as far as New York City.

We departed England in early May 1946. My parents saw Susan and me off at London Airport. As we embarked on our new life—Susan at my hand and another baby inside me—a haunting question lingered: *"How would I raise two children without their father?"*

I was attempting to be a good and strong mother by following the child-rearing teaching of Truby King, who was a popular physician and health reformer from New Zealand. The theory was very strict. There was no feeding on demand—you only fed babies every four hours even from the time they were first born—and you only took them out of their crib to hold them for a little while during what was called "mothering hour" around 4:00 p.m. Trying to adhere to this schedule on our journey made the flight very challenging—for Susan and me, and for everyone else on board.

Henry's grandmother and uncle and aunt came from Boston to meet Susan and me when we landed at LaGuardia Airport. They delivered us to the hotel and then left immediately. There we were in New York City at the Park Lane Hotel on Central Park, where Henry's father had booked us an overnight reservation. We knew no one at all in the city.

The next afternoon, at what would be English teatime, I went to the lounge of the hotel and asked for some tea. The waitress brought me a teapot, a cup, and a tea bag. I'd never seen a tea bag before and I didn't know what to do with it. I tried to pour what I expected to be tea from the pot but discovered it was only hot water. When I asked the waitress for some milk, she brought me a glass of cold milk. I thought, *"What do I do with this?"* I wanted milk for my tea, not to drink. I realized right then that this was a very different place with very different customs.

When I called my father-in-law to inquire about the next leg of our journey, he told me he had not yet been able to secure tickets for us. He instructed me to stay put and he would let me know when more flight arrangements were made.

So I went to the main lobby and spoke to the clerk, informing him that we needed to stay at least one additional night.

"I'm sorry, Madame," he said. "Your room has already been rented."

I asked if he had another room, and he replied simply, "No. I'm sorry."

Now, I was really frightened. I didn't know where to go or what to do. I was completely alone, and now I had visions of sitting outside the hotel with my little Susan and all our belongings.

I was also anxious because of the pregnancy. I wanted to fly on to Denver as soon as possible because in those days they didn't let you fly pregnant after a certain time. I don't think the planes were as well pressurized as they are today.

So, I sat in the lobby sort of shocked, and wondering *"What on earth should I do?"* I wouldn't say it was a prayer, but I did cry out in my heart.

Suddenly, it dropped into my mind that Henry had had a college roommate from New York City who was now an editor at *Time/Life*. His name was Hal Butterfield. I was able to find his phone number and I called him.

I told Hal I was Henry's widow and about my situation. He was so kind and he came right away and took Susan and me to his wife at their apartment. He said he would work on a flight to Denver for us, and with his connections he got us on a plane the very next day. I was so happy to be traveling on.

We arrived in Denver on May 8, 1946.

Coming to America, I felt as though I descended into my darkest days (1946 to 1948). I had never traveled out of England before, and once we landed in the United States, I found myself living in a strange land with strange customs, and a family I didn't know.

Life in America would revolve around living with Henry's father, Holbrook "Hoke" Mahn, and sister, Marion, in Denver, Colorado. They were Denver society. Actually, I didn't know Marion would also be living there. It was only a three-bedroom apartment and one of those bedrooms was for the housekeeper.

At first Marion went in with her father, and Susan and I took her room. A month later she got married and moved out, leaving Susan and me with Hoke.

Henry's father could be quite difficult to live with, and life was trying. My main focus was to be strong and to raise my children the best way I could.

Hoke was also a very tall, handsome man (like Henry), and he was very well off financially. He was an engineer, also having graduated from Harvard. His business had taken off after he designed and patented the Band-It high-pressure hose clamp. Now you see them all around the world on telephone and utility poles.

At times I found Hoke's habits very strange. Every day he ate lunch at the University Club and often in the evening he would come home and say he wanted only popcorn for dinner when I was ready to cook. After Marion moved out, I told Hoke we didn't need the housekeeper because I could do the cooking and cleaning, and he was fine with that.

In October, I gave birth to my Holbrook. Life became more demanding and Hoke's spontaneity became more challenging to accommodate. Sometimes, in the evening, he would come home and announce, "I think it would be nice to drive down to Colorado Springs for supper tonight."

I would ask, "With the children?"

He would reply, "Oh, yes! We'll just put them in the car."

For this type of outing, I thought I should pack an overnight bag. It was a 70-mile trip one way and in England that was considered an overnight stay.

But Hoke would say, "Oh, no! We'll just come back after dinner."

My strict child-rearing regimen became more stressed and challenging, but Hoke had no comprehension that it was difficult to travel like that. To me, this new lifestyle remained very foreign.

Another real tension was that I was not allowed to grieve the loss of Henry. Hoke was afraid I would cry a lot. He complained to Marion that he wouldn't know what to do with me if I cried. Instead, I tried my best to always put forward a good "stiff upper lip" as the English do anyway. All of it—leaving England, settling in Colorado, raising my children on my own—occurred in that first year without Henry. There were so many unknowns and I felt so very deeply alone.

Yet, there was also plenty to distract. Life with the Mahns presented a full social calendar. In those days after Hoke's wife had passed, there were a lot of women interested in him. Once I arrived on the scene, Hoke usually wanted me to go along to dinner parties or cocktail parties to be a good judge of these women. It was quite amusing. These ladies, some who were quite high society, would be trying to win my favor by giving me gifts for the baby.

Thankfully, in 1947, while still living with my father-in-law, my mother came to help care for Holbrook—we called him Billy when he was young. Henry had told me, if we had a boy, to name him William after the man, Bill Gardner, who managed the restaurant at the White Hall that was bombed in East Grinstead. So, I named him William Holbrook Mahn.

Somewhat fatefully, that November, Hoke and I attended a symphony fund drive at 200 Cherry Street, the residence of Jean and George Cranmer. Mr. Cranmer was a politician in the public works; Mrs. Cranmer was a central figure in the development and support of the Denver Symphony. We arrived early to the cocktail party, and the maid put us in the living room to wait for the other guests to begin arriving. I remember so clearly turning to Hoke and saying, "Good gracious, it looks like a church in here. It's amazing. I could never live in a place like this!"

I didn't meet Chap Cranmer at that party, but I did see the portrait of him in uniform—the one that now hangs in my home. I did meet his sister, Sylvia, and she asked me to help with the symphony drive in the Cheesman Park area where we lived. This was one of the oldest neighborhoods in Denver—full of mansions at the time. I would go door-to-door asking people to support or renew their subscription to the symphony—it was easy for me because I went to the park often with the children. Little by little my new life began to take shape.

CHAPTER THREE

Wonderful Dancer

He was too quiet and not very tall—that's all I thought of Chappell Cranmer when I first saw him at a party at the Cranmer home. I had no interest. He didn't make a good first impression, and I had no desire to meet him. There he was wearing a light grey suit and white socks. He had just come from California where he was working for the California Electric Power Company, which his grandfather had started.

It was 1947, and I was back at the house at 200 Cherry Street, having been invited for Sylvia Cranmer's birthday party on Christmas Eve. Denver life in those days was society life—a continual whirl of parties and functions. This was a whole new world for me as my family had been very middle class in England. But this was the life into which I was introduced when I came to the United States.

The following year at a large party in honor of Hoke's second marriage, my mum and I were both present. She was visiting from England for what would be an 18-month stay. Not surprisingly, Chap was there, although we were each with other dates. He had stayed on in Denver from the previous year after breaking his ankle while skating.

My mother met Chap that night, before he and I were formally introduced, and she was captivated. She spent almost the entire evening talking to him. Once back home, she went on and on about this perfect gentleman—so charming! Apparently, there was so much with which to be impressed: his knowledge of almost any topic from history to music to art, plus, stories of his travels. Who shouldn't be impressed? Still, I wasn't.

I had no interest in serious dating. My first husband, Henry, had died just over two years before, and I had only dated occasionally.

When Chap first called to take me out on a date, I declined. He called again.

My mother encouraged me saying, "Betty, I think you'll like him." I finally agreed to our first date at the end of June 1948 mainly to please her.

Chap took me dancing at the Park Lane Hotel near the Denver Country Club. I remember being so nervous. I had no idea what we would talk about. Even though mother had found him to be so fascinating, I still viewed him as too quiet and reserved.

These were the old days of rumbas, polkas, tangos, waltzes and the fox trot. Oh, what a wonderful dancer Chap proved himself to be—so light on his feet. I loved to dance, and I learned so much from Chap. I felt as light as a feather.

When he took me home that first night, he was a perfect gentleman— opening the car door and shaking my hand—simply thanking me for a nice evening. *Now* I was impressed.

Chap kept calling and we continued to date. On the Fourth of July we attended the Yellow Rose Ball in Central City, about 30 miles west of Denver in the front-range of the Rocky Mountains. It was our third date and we went along with the British Consul stationed in Denver, Bill Marchant, and his wife, Diane. It was a magical evening. As Chap took me to the door that night he kissed me goodnight.

When we were first dating, Chap was fetching me and bringing me home to the Marchant's home. My mother and I were staying with them to care for their young son while Mrs. Marchant recuperated from surgery.

It was at their home that Chap told me he wanted to pursue a relationship. I was still very hesitant. I enjoyed being with him, but I didn't know if I wanted to consider the relationship to be a serious one.

Shortly after the Yellow Rose Ball, Chap began inviting me quite regularly to dinner at the Cranmer home at 200 Cherry, which today faces

Cranmer Park. We attended the symphony often and also went to performances at Red Rocks Amphitheatre, which Chap's father was instrumental in developing.

At the end of July, Chap proposed and I was quick to say, "No." I didn't think I was ready—didn't really feel that I knew Chap well enough.

Chap could be a very focused man, and he persisted. He was confident in our relationship and wanted us to marry while my mother was still with us in Denver (her visa was due to expire in October). My logical response to his line of reasoning was that she could simply come back in another three years, and we could marry then. I was not in a rush. Actually, I believe I was still very much in love with Henry. It seemed all too difficult, so I put Chap off.

My mother, on the other hand, was not so easily put off. She believed Chap would make a wonderful husband for me, and a good father for Susan and Billy. It's funny because Chap didn't really spend any time with the children before we married, but my mother just knew his character. Chap's parents were also strongly in favor of marriage for Chap and me.

My mother and I continued staying at the Marchant's home through the rest of the summer. In this way, Bill Marchant got to know, or at least to observe, Chap, as we continued to date.

In August, Chap proposed marriage for the second time. This time I said, "Yes." We were sitting on the couch in the living room of the Marchant's home. Later, when I told Bill, he acted surprised and asked why he had not been consulted regarding Chap's intentions. It was all very nice and fatherly even though Bill was only a few years older than I was.

The wedding was set for October 15, 1948, at four o'clock in the afternoon at St. Martin's Chapel next to St. John's Episcopal Cathedral. Between our engagement and wedding the social whirl was in full swing. There were many, many parties—several each week.

Dean Roberts, who confirmed me in the Episcopal Church as an adult (I had never been confirmed growing up), performed the ceremony. My mother was in the front row with my father who flew over for the occasion. Marion, my first sister-in-law, was my matron of honor and Chap's sister was my bride's maid. Chap's best man was John R. "Jack" Durrance, his good friend who had saved his life on their heroic attempt to climb K2 in 1939.

Walking down the aisle, I remember asking myself, *"Do I really know this man?"* It was a step of faith in a way.

Our wedding reception was held at the classic Italian-style Cranmer home. Hundreds of people attended—most of whom I didn't even know. That was to be our life in those days, very much caught up in the society life of Denver.

Chap continued to woo me as we honeymooned in British Columbia. We flew to Seattle and drove all the way up to Lake Louise and Banff. Every inch of the countryside was breathtaking. On our way back down, we ferried over and stayed at the elegant Empress Hotel on Victoria Island. I loved the English influence. It was wonderful for me in every way. We had tea every afternoon and danced and danced and danced, nearly every evening. Life was lovely.

When we were first married, Chap was working as a stockbroker, but his business wasn't doing well. He really wasn't a salesman. With the influence of his uncle, Harry Cranmer, who was working in uranium in Utah and doing pretty well, Chap also went into the business.

We lived at 200 Cherry. Chap's mother wanted us to stay in their home with my first pregnancy because they were going to be away travelling. As the babies kept coming, we stayed on. Allen came in 1949, and then Bruce in 1950, followed by Jeanie in 1952, and Forrest in 1955. Soon we filled the second floor.

Chap was a quiet and strict father. Our young family was active out-doors, following Chap's passion for skiing and climbing mountains. In the winters, we skied Arapahoe Basin nearly every week, and in the summer months, we went camping and hiking. No matter what the activity, all of our children went along in tow.

But by 1955, Chap was not well and had been rapidly losing weight, get-ting down as low as 98 pounds. Whatever he ate was going straight through him and he just wasn't getting nourishment. Still living at the Cranmer home in Denver, we were feeding him rich food to try to keep or put weight on him. Later, we learned this was the worst thing for him.

His mother thought he was overworked, so she encouraged him to close up shop for a while, and she sent us to La Jolla, California, for rest and to renew Chap's health.

I was afraid he was going to die. I began thinking *"I'll be a widow again—now with six children!"*

It was at that time, I first read a book by Norman Vincent Peale that Chap's mother had given us. There was a chapter in it on widowhood. I read it, and at the end it included the Scripture: "I can do everything through Him who gives me strength" (Philippians 4:13, NIV). I wrote that down, and I began to write down other verses to help me take courage. I wasn't a be-liever in God, but I thought, *"Well, if there is a God, I certainly will need his help."*

I don't remember praying at the time. Chap may have been praying—he did bring a Bible with us to La Jolla—but if he was, he didn't tell me. Still, there was a very real sense that God must have been watching over us.

We made the long drive from Colorado to California in a station wagon with our six children and no air conditioner. Chap was clear to say right off, "It's going to be hot, so I don't want any complaints."

When we got to the Mojave Desert, Holbrook (Billy) was sitting up front with his Dad and me, and at one point he turned to his Father and said in a calm, quiet sort of voice, "Daddy, do you think it's hot now?" Chap replied, "Maybe." Then we turned off to get gas, and Chap bought everyone an ice cream treat. We looked at the temperature and it read 120 degrees.

Finally, we arrived in La Jolla with all its coastal beauty, and we were there from August to October 1955. It was a wonderful time. We stayed at the La Jolla Tennis and Beach Club. When we walked out of our front door, there was the beach right in front of us. Chap spent a lot of time reading and resting, and the children and I played on the beach endlessly and happily.

When we returned to Denver, Chap's good friend and best man, Jack Durrance, called and told us he had found a physician at the Veteran's Administration Hospital who thought he knew what might be wrong with Chap.

Chap had had a long history of illness. He had often been sick as a child and young man. When he was in the Marines they had done several tests on him. They thought his chronic illnesses could be caused by all kinds of different things, including possibly amebic dysentery.

Once he may have had malaria, and when he attempted the climb on K2, he suffered a pulmonary edema, which kept him at base camp. Jack was one of the leaders on that climb and he stayed with Chap and breathed into him in order to keep him alive because they didn't carry oxygen tanks in those days.

So we went to the Veteran's Hospital. Right off the doctor told Chap, "I think you have sprue." He kept him in the hospital for a couple of weeks, putting him through several more tests. In the end, the diagnosis was sprue (celiac disease), which is an autoimmune disorder of the small intestine causing an inability to digest the gluten in grains, as well as certain fats.

We took him off of all breads and other foods containing gluten, and put him on fish, skim milk and potatoes. Chap began gaining a pound a day.

Even with the adjustment in his diet, he had to remain very careful because he could experience flair ups periodically. It was a wonderful relief to watch Chap regain health.

After Chap's illness, we moved into our own home at 120 Race and he invested in the Portable X-ray Company. He didn't know anything about portable x-ray at first, but he knew people who were running the business and needed financing. So he invested and worked at the business for a year or so when the owner, a young man in his 30s, died suddenly of a heart attack.

Now Chap had the business on his hands while he was still learning. He decided to buy out the owner's widow and ran the business for several more years (from 1956 into the 1960s). He had good people working for him, but he wasn't making any money.

By about 1957, things were already getting tough with the business. I can still see him now, sitting in the kitchen of our home near the country club. He looked at me and said, "I am at the end of my rope."

By this time I had gained a strong faith in God and Chap's declaration did not frighten me. I simply said, "Oh, great—now we can give our lives to God."

I remember I went on and on, with all sorts of ideas, including I think the possibility of becoming missionaries. I told Chap, "Sweetie, we could sell the house." I didn't care where we lived or what we did—I just wanted Chap to be happy and fulfilled.

He looked at me and said, "Oh, dear! Not only am I at the end of my rope—now my wife is having these wild ideas."

Still, it was at that time Chap first said to me, "Perhaps we should start going to church." We began attending regularly at St. John's Episcopal Cathedral. We took all six children—Forrest, the youngest, was just two years old—so they were raised going to church. Shortly after we began attending, we became very much involved.

CHAPTER FOUR

Why Did They Need God?

I was already teaching Sunday school at St. John's Cathedral when I first got involved with the women's reading group. We met socially with many of the women who attended this group. Chap had grown up with most of the people we now mixed with at church.

A woman who would become a very good friend, Betty Ashley, led the reading group, and even though it was not a Bible study, she would begin the meetings with prayer.

She said the most wonderful prayers. Sometimes I was so amazed I would open my eyes to see if she was reading them, but she wasn't—her eyes were closed. I thought she must have memorized them—they were so beautiful.

After a while I asked her, "Betty, where do you learn these prayers?"

"I don't," she said, "I just close my eyes and the Lord gives me the words."

Then she said, "If you really want to understand, you can come to a Bible study with me on Wednesdays."

The only times I remember praying to God when I was quite young was when I played sports at school, what we called netball or basketball. When we traveled to the games by bus I would sometimes get motion sickness because we loved to sit in the upper seating of those double-decker buses.

If I began to feel sick, I would pray, *"Please don't let me get sick—and if I don't get sick I'll give some of my pocket money to the waifs and strays."* That was how it worked.

In regard to church, I just wanted to be confirmed because my brothers were able to take communion and I wasn't. I guess I believed there was a God, but I did not know Him.

After several of the women from the Bible study invited me to lunch to talk about God, I went to the group with Betty. That's where I came into a larger circle of wealthy, well-educated women who all seemed to know God in a very personal way. It was amazing to me. Holly Coors, whom I knew, was there along with Harriett Corbin, who was translating a lot of Corrie ten Boom's writing.

At that first meeting, it was quite surprising to me to have the leader, Miriam Conklin, ask me boldly, "Are you saved?" She was a Presbyterian woman who had come to practice a very free expression of what we would call the gifts of the Holy Spirit.

I responded quite innocently by asking, "What do you mean?"

"Well then you're not," she replied.

Miriam told me that I needed to say the sinner's prayer and I said, "Fine." I didn't know what I was doing really, but I had no objections.

The question I could not escape—the curiosity that really led me to trust Christ initially, even though I didn't understand it all was quite simply—*"Why did they need God?"* I saw that these were extremely wealthy women. They were all college educated. They had everything and anything they wanted. They could buy anything. Do anything. Go anywhere.

I thought as many people do that you have to have a big need—something that drives you to give up and give your life to God. I learned that is just not true. These women didn't *need* anything.

They were believers in God from many different denominations. I witnessed the fullness of life they experienced, and it wasn't because of their money or education. They were full of God and full of His Holy Spirit.

Betty Ashley, the woman I went with to the group, was one who would become quite close to me in the faith. She was a friend and mentor in spiritual things—a beautiful person—and I loved her.

As I surrendered my life to God, I found such complete freedom and peace. I wasn't worrying. I was praying. Chap saw this and recognized it for what it was. He saw that I was a changed and changing person. Shortly after I became involved with the women's Bible study, Chap joined the Full Gospel Businessmen's Association, where he was exposed to the key teachers in the charismatic movement of the 1960s.

Chap and I became more involved in the movement. We sat under the teaching of people like Dennis Bennett, an Episcopal priest who authored *Nine O'clock in the Morning*, and Derek Prince, who had been a professor of logic at Cambridge University before the war, and had written many scholarly books.

About a year after I started attending the Bible study, I experienced another important introduction in this new spiritual life into which I had stepped. I was with a few of the women, lingering after one of our Bible study sessions. These women were full of the Holy Spirit of God. They were bold. They just came right out and asked me if I wanted to receive the fullness of the Holy Spirit.

I said, "Fine." I was pretty matter of fact about it. If they had it, I might as well have it. That was my thinking. I didn't think I needed it particularly. I was very practical. Yet, these women were dynamic and full of joy, so it was very attractive.

Several times before, they had asked me if I wanted them to pray for me and I had always responded, "Well, there's nothing wrong with me." This time it was different. I still didn't feel there was anything particularly wrong or missing from my life, but I was drawn to what they experienced in their spiritual lives.

As we sat together after the study, Betty Ashley came toward me to pray for me, as we say, "with the laying on of hands." This is simply to put your hands on another person's shoulders or back while you pray for them. It's a form of prayer that represents an extension of God's touching us.

Well, Betty didn't even reach me before she collapsed very gently onto the floor, she was so full with God's Spirit. I didn't understand this at the time, but I knew something significant and powerful and true was happening.

Immediately, I started praying in the Spirit and felt a peace and freedom that I had never known before. It was as if my whole life was right there before me, and before God, and He fully accepted me. It was an experience of utter joy.

Shortly after that experience, I had the opportunity to meet Corrie ten Boom for the first time. She was speaking at a gathering near Colorado Springs. I went with Millie Wykstra, a friend and fellow teacher with whom I was working in the Head Start program. We had heard that this little Dutch woman, an evangelist from Holland, was speaking and that she had hidden Jews from the Nazis during World War II.

At the end of Corrie's talk, she invited people to come to the front of the room if they had anything they wanted, in prayer, to give back to God. This was a symbolic exercise, a sort of "putting on the altar" or releasing back to God something or someone in one's life for whom you were very grateful and yet you wanted to trust God with and not hold control over.

As I stood at the front of the church, I silently asked God what He wanted me to release to Him. I felt impressed quite strongly that it was my family—all my family—Chap and our six children. So, I did that. In prayer, I gave them back to God. It felt a bit like the story in the Bible of Abraham laying Isaac on the altar. I did it in a childlike way. My faith was childlike then—and remains very much that way today.

While driving back to Denver, Millie said, "You don't have to tell me, but I'm curious—what did you put on the altar tonight?"

I told her, "I was very impressed to lay my family on the altar."

She was quite shocked and said, "Suppose God takes them all?"

"Well," I said, "I think the Lord will sustain me."

I knew I hadn't thought it through. As I said, it was a very childlike act. I just wanted to do what God wanted for me and then to trust Him with whatever would happen. It was a point of surrender. I wanted nothing in my life to come before God.

During Chap's long illness several years before, he read the Bible. As my life began to change and I became more involved in Bible study and prayer, he noticed. Step by step, from his illness on, he was being drawn closer to God as well.

From 1964 to 1966, we attended Full Gospel Businessmen's meetings in Denver. Chap enjoyed these gatherings of professionals—they were successful in business and yet they were very devoted to the spiritual components in their lives.

Particularly, Chap respected Lee Ashley, my friend Betty's husband. Lee was bright, intelligent and an officer at a large bank. Chap reasoned if Lee was involved in these gatherings then they must be okay.

On one occasion, Chap and I traveled to Colorado Springs to meet for lunch with Hattie Corbin and Corrie ten Boom. After our meal, Corrie prayed for him to receive the fullness of the Holy Spirit. He did not pray in the Spirit at that time, but as we drove home he kept commenting that it was quite warm in the car, which it wasn't. Quietly, I thought he was just being blessed by the fullness of the Spirit.

On this spiritual journey Chap and I shared, we also began to open our home to many traveling speakers who would come through Denver with the charismatic movement. We met people who had been instantly healed of drug addiction, as well as many others—they all made a profound impact on us.

Being Episcopalian, we were particularly encouraged by Dennis Bennett, who as an Episcopal priest spoke of his own charismatic experience. The first time we heard him, he walked out to speak wearing his priest's collar. Immediately, we felt at ease. His well-reasoned and yet impassioned message was a powerful testimony.

In the early 1960s the movement of the Holy Spirit was strong in people's lives—you had to be careful then as you do now to listen to authentic, godly teachers—and Chap and I were happy to be involved in that movement.

Chap was still working with the Portable X-ray Company. He hoped to get out of it, and he began to pray for God's guidance. Often he would get away to the mountains to pray, and on these outings he found that another desire was growing in his heart—he felt he was being led by God to go into the ministry.

We were now attending a smaller parish, St. Philip and St. James Episcopal Church in Denver. The priest there, Father Vern Myers, was Spirit-filled and he counseled Chap to seek confirmation of his ministry calling. He encouraged him to go before a commission of ministers and then to the bishop of the diocese. In the Episcopal Church all this was necessary for Chap to receive approval to attend seminary and pursue the priesthood, and it was all quite life changing. We felt ourselves stepping out into unchartered waters.

Around the late 1950s, I shared with Chap that I wanted to have another baby. Originally, I had wanted 12 children. He said, "We do have to educate the children we have," and he encouraged me to pursue opportunities to be involved with more children outside of our home. So I went for certification in early childhood development and then worked with the Head Start program in the Denver public schools.

School picture, 1929

My mother, Dorothy

My father, Alfred

*Here I am at five years old
with my brothers (l to r),
Cyril (11) and Bill (6);
in front is our cousin,
Teddy (2)*

*(l to r) Bill (17) and
Cyril (22) with me (16)*

*Walking with my father in
Morecambe, during my air
force training, 1941*

Henry on an outing in
East Grinstead during his
convalescence

Henry, with his new legs,
climbing into a Spitfire for
flight training, 1943

Henry and me at our
wedding at St. Swithin's
Church, 1944

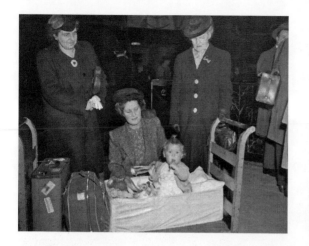

Susan and me being greeted by Henry's relatives at LaGuardia Airport, 1946

Jean and George Cranmer's home at 200 Cherry Street in Denver

The living room at 200 Cherry

Chap and me at our wedding reception at the Cranmer home, 1948

Our family in La Jolla, 1954 – (l to r) Bruce, Chap, Allen, "Billy," Jeanie, me, and Susan (Forrest was not yet born)

Our children in the garden at 200 Cherry, 1957 – (l to r) Susan, "Billy," Allen, Bruce, Jeanie, and Forrest

The family skiing at Arapahoe Basin – (l to r) Allen, Susan, Jeanie standing on my skis, "Billy," and Chap with Bruce on his skis

Teaching with Head Start at the Lincoln Housing Project in Denver, 1967

In the 1960s when I became involved with the women's Bible study at St. John's Cathedral

Allen leaving for Vietnam from our home at 120 Race Street, 1969 — (l to r) Jeanie, Bruce, Allen, Holbrook, Susan, Forrest, and me

Forrest skiing at Winter Park Ski Resort, after the surgery that left him partially paralyzed, 1978

Forrest graduating Colorado College, 1977

Chap and me in the 1980s

On our bike tour of
France, 1985

Susan and me,
Christmas 1994

My surprise 80th
birthday party, 2001 –
(l to r) Susan, Holbrook,
Allen, me, Bruce, and
Jeanie

With my brother,
Bill, 2010

Robb Rankin and me at the CASEY
award ceremony, 2007

Church portrait, 2008

CHAPTER FIVE

Planted in High Places

Once Chap knew he was to go to seminary and pursue the priesthood in the Episcopal Church, he went to see the bishop who asked him where he intended to study. Chap had done his research and he told the bishop he wanted to go to the Church Divinity School of the Pacific (CDSP) in Berkeley, California. He knew it to be an excellent seminary, but this was also a practical decision for Chap. His sister, Sylvia, lived in Berkeley, so he knew he could stay with her, which would help keep costs down.

Initially, the bishop said, "No," and Father Myers from St. Philip and St. James possessed very little confidence that Chap would receive a positive answer from the bishop. Typically, all the candidates for the priesthood from our diocese attended Seabury-Western Theological Seminary in Evanston, Illinois.

Chap persevered in his discussions with the bishop, and at one point the bishop asked him to explain his desire more fully. "Why would you want to go to a place like that?" he asked. The bishop's disapproval was not so much about the school itself. He was unsure of it simply because he had no other experience with sending candidates for the priesthood so far away.

Chap explained his reasoning very thoroughly: There would be a savings in cost because of the availability of housing with his sister, and we would better preserve our limited income for the family's needs as I would stay home in Colorado and carry on with regular daily life for myself and our six children. Finally, he told the bishop quite frankly that he felt that CDSP was precisely where the Lord wanted him to study.

The bishop gave his approval and when Chap stepped out of that meeting Father Myers told him he had made history.

Chap entered the two-year Master of Divinity program at CDSP. He wasn't interested in studying longer to get a Ph.D.—his intention was to return to Colorado as soon as he could and begin serving as a vicar in the Episcopal Church.

The reason we did not all go out to California while Chap was in seminary was that we felt it would be too disruptive to the children's lives and to my work. However, during those few years Chap was away, our lives would change dramatically: Forrest would be diagnosed with a brain tumor, and Allen would be called up to serve in Vietnam. I carried a lot on my shoulders.

Thanks to the generosity of Chap's father, I also received a steady supply of airline tickets and was able to fly out and be with Chap pretty regularly. Chap had driven to California on his motorcycle, so when I was there we would tour all over the Bay Area on that cycle.

After completing seminary, Chap was first ordained as a deacon at St. John's Episcopal Cathedral in Denver on June 24, 1969. Right after ordination, he was sent to serve in two small parishes in Grand County—the Episcopal Church of St. John the Baptist in Granby and Trinity Church in Kremmling. (In the Episcopal Church one first serves as deacon for at least six months before being installed as a priest or vicar.)

In the first year of his service, Chap kept a small apartment in Granby, which is about 95 miles northwest of Denver. I remained in Denver with the children mostly because Jeanie was still a senior in high school. On weekends, I would go up to the mountains to be with Chap and to attend services.

I will never forget the Sunday Chap was set to give his first sermon as deacon. At around 7:00 in the morning, as we were getting dressed, our good friends and neighbors in the apartment complex came over to tell us Forrest was having a grand mal seizure. Bruce and Susan, who were with

Forrest in Denver, had called our neighbors because we did not have a telephone in the apartment.

Forrest wasn't breathing, and the ambulance had been called from Denver General. Before this, Forrest had only experienced a petit mal. Chap and I felt caught—we were almost two hours. Chap felt we needed to go ahead to church, pray and trust Forrest to God.

I remember it all so clearly. We drove to Trinity Church in Kremmling, about 35 miles west of Granby. When we arrived, we called to check on the situation with Forrest but didn't get through.

The service began and I sat in the front pew. There weren't many people there that day due to bad weather. The Scripture reading was from the Gospel of John about the Apostle Peter walking on the water to Jesus. It impressed me quite strongly.

As Chap was preaching, I felt he was speaking directly to me—to both of us. We didn't know whether Forrest was alive or not, and we needed faith and trust in God.

I thought, *"Lord, this is exactly what we're doing right now—walking on the water to you. All we have to do is keep our eyes on you—otherwise we're going to sink."*

After the service, we called again and learned that Forrest was all right. He had started breathing and the ambulance had actually been called off, so he had not gone to the hospital. Of course, we were incredibly relieved.

Six months later, on Christmas Eve, Chap was ordained as a priest at a 6:00 p.m. service at St. Philip and St. James Episcopal Church. It was amazing because he was set to do his first service as a vicar that same night in Granby at the 11:00 p.m. Christmas service. In a terrible blizzard, we drove up the mountain for the service with Susan, Jeanie and Forrest in the car. We were slipping and sliding all over the road, but Chap kept a steady hand at the wheel, and we arrived safely in time for the service.

In 1970, we bought the house at 55 W Garnet Avenue and moved full-time to Granby. Forrest was the only child left at home to move with us (he was in 9th grade). Jeanie graduated high school and went off to Colorado College. Allen joined her there, when he returned from Vietnam. Susan was at the University of Colorado at Denver. Holbrook was teaching at Denver Country Day/Kent, and Bruce was studying at the University of Colorado at Boulder and skiing on the ski team.

Chap settled into his duties as vicar, and never looked beyond Granby to other places to serve. He believed very strongly that we should bloom where we were planted. For us, this was in the high places of the Colorado Rocky Mountains.

In 1981, in addition to his regular duties, Chap began ministering at a small chapel in Winter Park, a town about 20 miles away. He held Saturday evening services for the skiers, tourists, and other weekend visitors to the county. This chapel (a small cabin) was donated to the Episcopal Diocese of Colorado by a developer in the area named Victor Vestman. Chap was influential in the chapel being named for St. Colomba after he visited the small island of Iona, off the coast of Scotland, where the Irishman first evangelized in the 6th century. Chap continued to hold services at the chapel for another 15 years after his retirement from St. John's.

CHAPTER SIX

Our Unpredictable Life with Forrest

It was sort of cool and overcast that Christmas Eve Day, 1970. There weren't many people on the slopes as, I imagine, they were busy doing other things like finishing holiday preparations.

I didn't really want to go skiing, having plenty of things to do myself before the service that night and our family gathering the next day. Forrest really wanted to ski and nobody else could go with him. So, we set the early part of the day aside and skied the slopes at Winter Park Ski Resort.

Forrest's mood was typically good—he was such a happy-go-lucky person. He was fine that day, and just thought it would be nice to do a few runs. He could be quite stubborn and wanted his own way in many things, but this time there was no fuss.

Usually, Chap was the one who skied with Forrest, but this was my turn with him. It was just the two of us, and Forrest was really enjoying himself. We didn't often ski right together as he skied much faster than I did, but I was enjoying myself as well.

Because it was Christmas Eve, I thought we wouldn't stay very late so we didn't even take a break for lunch. In the morning, we skied a few runs near Cranmer Cutoff. Then, around lunchtime, we got on the chairlift up by Snoasis, the restaurant half way up the big ski mountain. In those days there was a double chair lift—one of the older ones that had no safety bar.

We had just gotten on, and we were riding it up over Cranmer Cutoff. The lift went up quite steeply right at the beginning, so almost immediately you were about 30 feet above the ground and the ski run was right below.

Right then, Forrest had a seizure. He was sitting on my left-hand side and all of a sudden he started stiffening up. I felt him slipping out of the chair and I couldn't hold him. He slid right down and out of the chair—taking one of my poles with him. As I looked down, I could see he was face down in the snow.

There was never any warning with these things. He could be in the middle of a sentence and have a seizure and then he was just unconscious. There was no fatigue or distress to act as a warning. Most typically, Forrest would just moan, hold his breath and fall backwards. Then he would pass out and be out for an hour or so, depending on whether or not it was a petit or grand mal.

That's what had just happened, but this time from 30 feet high!

I thought *"Oh, Lord!"* My mind went right back to that time with Corrie when I had surrendered what was dearest to me—my husband and all of my children. In my heart, I had figuratively laid them all on the altar before God several years before, trusting each of them to God's care.

So when Forrest fell off the chair lift, I said in my heart to the Lord, *"Is this the time that you're going to take him?"* I just cried out to God to send somebody there to take care of him, and I once again surrendered Forrest into God's hands. Immediately, a wonderful peace came over me, and I started praying in the Spirit. I prayed throughout the duration of the ride on the chairlift, which took another 20 minutes.

When I got to the top the attendant said to me, "Are you the person who had someone fall off the chairlift?"

"Yes!" I said.

He asked what had happened, and I told him Forrest had had a seizure. When I asked if Forrest was alive, the attendant had no information he could give me.

So I skied down with my one pole to where Forrest's impression was in the snow where he had fallen, but the area had already been roped off and Forrest was gone. The ski patrol had apparently gotten to him quickly; they loaded him up and were already taking him down on a toboggan to the ski patrol hut.

I asked some people who were nearby, "Was he alive?"

Somebody answered, "We heard that a doctor was the first one to get to him and turned his face so he could breathe. That's all we know."

Oh, what thankfulness I felt—that was what I was most concerned about while I was up on the chairlift. I knew he needed to be turned over right away so he wouldn't suffocate in the snow.

Somewhat relieved, I hurriedly skied on down and caught up to Forrest and the others on the toboggan. Excitedly, I asked, "Is he alive?"

"Yes!" they answered.

They explained that Forrest seemed confused to them when they first spoke to him.

"In what way?" I asked.

They said, "We couldn't really get his name from him—he seemed confused or disoriented. When we asked, he just kept saying 'forest,' and then 'Cranmer.'"

I said, "No, he's not confused—his name is *Forrest Cranmer*."

That solved the mystery for them. The mistake was understandable as Forrest had fallen in the trees on Cranmer Cutoff, and there had been no way for them to know that he was actually a member of the Cranmer family. It was a good bit of humor in the midst of the whole ordeal.

I was just so thankful Forrest was alive, but it took quite a long time for him to come around. From the time I skied down from the top of the run to where I found him on the trail with the ski patrol, it was probably half an hour to three quarters of an hour.

As soon as we got to the small warming hut (in 1970 there was no clinic and there were no doctors there), I called Chap and told him what had happened. By this time Forrest was coming around and he was much more lucid.

The ski patrol who had brought Forrest down thought he had a wonderful sense of humor. He just kept trying to explain himself, and when he said he was Forrest Cranmer, they said, "You're related to George?"

Of course this was the absolute truth because it was George Cranmer, Chap's father, who had developed the Winter Park ski area, and for whom Cranmer Cutoff was named.

Forrest happily answered the patrolmen, "Yes, I'm his grandson." They all thought that was good fun, and Forrest so enjoyed chatting with them. I guess he was always talkative—like his mother. (It could also be told, here, that Forrest was named for Chap's older brother, Forrest Cranmer, who moved to France in 1970 and later settled permanently in England.)

Soon Chap arrived and we took Forrest to the hospital in Kremmling, where they x-rayed him and found out that he had also chipped a part of the bone on his ankle. The doctors told us he would have to spend the night in the hospital, which was very upsetting to Forrest. He didn't want to be there on Christmas Eve. He wanted to go home and to St. John's for the evening service, but there was no choice in the matter—he just had to stay.

When Forrest was coming out of a seizure, you never really knew how much he understood or remembered. A lot of the time, the day after a seizure, he wouldn't remember anything he had done or said. After his fall from the chairlift, he had no memory of it. That's what life was like with Forrest.

These sorts of experiences with Forrest began back in March 1969, just before Chap returned from seminary. Forrest had sort of fainted, having his first petit mal. Then, he had another episode shortly after.

By May, the doctors felt they should do a pneumoencephalogram (PEG) in order to get a better view of the brain. It was a painful procedure that drained the fluid from the brain and replaced it with air. Today, they would have performed an MRI or other non-invasive procedure to find the same results.

Chap was taking his finals at this time so he couldn't be with us. After the exams, the doctors informed me there was no hope. They had found an inoperable tumor on Forrest's brain. When they told us their diagnosis, I told them, "We have hope!"—I was holding on to the words of Psalm 41 that had come to me when I was praying in the hospital chapel:

"The Lord will sustain him on his sickbed and restore him from his bed of illness" (Psalm 41:3, NIV).

We always maintained hope with regard to Forrest's seizures. In 1970, he didn't experience a single seizure until the fall. The doctors had put him on Dilantin to help control them, although it seemed to have little effect. It calmed him some, but it didn't stop the seizures from occurring.

In the summer of 1970 Forrest and I traveled to Europe for a month, just the two of us. Chap's mother sent us, thinking it would be good for Forrest. We drove all around and had a wonderful time seeing sights and visiting friends, including Corrie ten Boom at her home in Holland. We enjoyed many adventures—seeing Salzburg and going down the Rhine River. We drove everywhere in a small Volkswagen Beetle. Forrest was fine the entire trip. It was a real gift.

Some of our best adventures occurred during the drive from Oberammergau to Salzburg and then on to Heidelberg. I was doing all the driving because Forrest didn't drive. Amazingly, we did everything without advance reservations.

At Oberammergau we had driven into town and found a lovely small hotel with beautiful flowers where we wanted to stay. I was so naive that when we first arrived and picked that hotel, I went in and just simply asked the proprietor for a nice room with two beds for Forrest and me. He had asked if we had reservations, and I told him very matter-of-factly, "No."

He said, "Madame, we are all booked and have been *for 10 years.* Don't you know this is the year of *The Passion Play* which is only performed every 10 years?" He was absolutely shocked at our presumption.

He suggested we go down to Unterammergau, a small village. So we went, but there was still no hotel space available.

Finally, a patron of one of the hotels where we inquired suggested a small chalet with bed and breakfast. It was run by a jolly, large woman who didn't speak a word of English. Even though I spoke no German, we managed to understand she had one room available.

To our surprise, we learned it was a small room up in a loft—a room with one large feather bed. I wasn't sure what to do, but it appeared that Forrest and I would have to sleep together. It seemed to be our only option—so we took in our things and got settled.

While at the first hotel in Oberammergau, we had also inquired about getting tickets for *The Passion Play*, which is an incredible theatrical production of the life and death of Jesus.

Once again, the hotel proprietor just looked shocked at our inquiry, telling us there were no tickets and there hadn't been any for some time. The play is performed continually over a period of several months, but only in the first year of every decade.

In the end, the proprietor gave us one more suggestion. He said, "Come back at 7:30 the morning of the day you hope to attend, and see if any tickets have been turned in by people who cannot use them."

We did just as we were told, and the very next day we found ourselves attending *The Passion Play*. It was an absolutely amazing experience.

Back at our chalet, communication with our innkeeper continued with great humor. Our dear host would speak to us in German, and we would speak back to her in English. Somehow we were quite successful in getting the croissants and coffee we desired for breakfast each morning. Lots of laughter accompanied every conversation.

The day we were to leave, this jovial German woman kept going on and on about Forrest. With the few German words I did understand I began to gather that she thought perhaps Forrest was my husband and not my son.

When this came to light, I began to say repeatedly, "Nein, nein—not mann, not mann—*kinder!*"

When she heard this she absolutely roared with laughter. We all did!

It had been a lovely two-day visit.

Soon, we were off on the next leg of our adventure—a drive to Salzburg to see all the castles and the movie locations for *The Sound of Music*. From there we planned to travel on to Heidelberg.

As with everywhere we journeyed, we went without reservations. In some towns there was no problem finding accommodations, but in others it was impossible.

This was the case in Düsseldorf, on the way to Heidelberg. We had driven a long distance that day, and I was very tired. We inquired at several hotels and found nothing. We drove from village to village, stopping to inquire for hotel availability. Nothing. Finally, as it began to get dark, I gave up and told Forrest we had no other option—we would find a rest stop and sleep in the car.

Well, the Volkswagen wasn't very big, so we just *sat up* in the car, and that was that. At three o'clock in the morning I woke up and told Forrest I thought it was getting light and that I didn't want to sleep anymore. I wanted to wash my face and clean my teeth in order to help me feel better, and then get on the road.

As I fumbled around in our luggage I couldn't find my overnight bag with my toiletries. I asked Forrest about it, but he just thought it was in the back of the car. We determined we must have left it at the hotel in Salzburg. I was more than a little panicked because in that bag was my beautiful sapphire engagement ring, my pearls, and all my jewelry. I knew we had to turn around immediately.

Even though we had covered many kilometers in the previous days, we had to retrace them now. When we arrived back in Salzburg, there was my bag still sitting in the lobby right where we had left it. No one had bothered with it. We were utterly amazed.

After a quick yogurt for breakfast, we got back on the road once again. Now, we were headed through Munich for the *third* time because we were determined to get to Heidelberg. There was a lot of construction and the going was quite slow. The work must have been for the upcoming Olympic games, which would be in Munich in 1972.

Having had very little sleep and doing all that extra driving back and forth, I told Forrest, "I don't care how much it costs tonight—when we get to Heidelberg we're going to have a bed to sleep in!" Of all things we found a Texaco Motel and enjoyed the very best night's sleep.

All of our journeys that summer seemed like faith stories. We felt God helped us at every turn. But the greatest part of it all was that Forrest did not experience one seizure throughout the entire summer's travel through Europe. So, when the seizures did return that November, Forrest was pretty discouraged. He had hoped, and we did too, that they were behind him.

For most of his young life, from age 14 on, seizures were commonplace for Forrest. When they occurred, Forrest would fall backwards, often hitting his head. Later, when he had surgery to remove the tumor and lost his hair due to the radiation, it was just amazing to see his baldhead covered with stitch marks from all the falls he had endured.

Still, Forrest always got on with life. He was always thankful and didn't speak much about his discouragement. He once said to me, "Mother, if I stopped to think of what could happen to me during the day, I would never get out of bed." Instead, he trusted God and went about his business. Some of the things he would do were terribly concerning for me, but that was Forrest. He exhibited no fear.

Often he would ride his bike from Granby to Grand Lake on the highway. That's a 15-mile trip one way. Usually, he did just fine, but there was the time I got a call from a local friend who found Forrest lying on the side of the road having had a seizure while he was riding. Experiences like that were common for us with Forrest, but his spirits were never dampened. At almost any event in his life he loved to exclaim, "I am just *so thank-full!*"

Forrest had always been a happy baby and a happy young boy. He came to faith in Christ at a very young age. He learned about Jesus at Sunday school and wanted to know Him, so one day he asked me to pray with him. He was only about five or six years old. He was full of joy.

In preschool, he absolutely loved his teacher, Mrs. Duffy. All of our children had gone to her. She was wonderful—a small, cuddly woman. One day, I remember trying to hurry Forrest along to get ready for school. Gently giving him a nudge, I said to him, "Oh come on Forrest, go along." He turned right around to me and said very calmly, "We don't push at Mrs. Duffy's." He was just three years old.

Forrest wanted to go to preschool when he was two years old because Jeanie was going. Mrs. Duffy said to let him come and try it just a couple of mornings each week for the summer. By September, he wanted to go every day.

I left the decision to Mrs. Duffy, and she decided to take him. So he was there for three years, and he absolutely loved it. They would have very special tea parties and he would come home telling me all about them.

On the very last day, after three years, I said to Forrest, "This is it—you have to go to kindergarten." I told him he would have to say goodbye to Mrs. Duffy, but he asked, "Why, Mummy?" I explained to him that he had to go to a big school. He was very earnest when he replied, "But Mummy, Mrs. Duffy can teach me because she knows *everything*."

Forrest graduated from Middle Park High School in Granby in 1973, and he was determined to go to college. He applied to Colorado College (CC) in Colorado Springs. To this day, it is a very special school with a wonderful administration and faculty. The school administration knew our family, because Jeanie and Allen had attended there at the same time. They also had special programs in place to accommodate Forrest's learning needs.

So Forrest was accepted and suddenly his dream was coming true—he was going away to college. This was a particularly difficult decision for me. I wasn't comfortable with him being so far away from Granby where everybody knew him. Chap was supportive, and so we decided to trust God with Forrest and allow him to go.

Once there, Forrest made all sorts of good friends. He joined a collegiate Christian group called Campus Life, and he pursued a degree in general studies that included religion, art and history.

He also enrolled in French, but this pursuit led to the discovery that whenever he had a seizure he would forget all the material he had just studied. With the large amount of memorization required for foreign language, it became apparent that Forrest would have to let go of this goal. Likewise, he also had to let go of the dream of driving, which he had held from the time he was quite young and would sit for hours behind the wheel of a parked car.

Other than those couple of things, Forrest pursued most any and every activity he found interesting, and his good friends at CC—students, professors and administrators—truly did look after him.

One night he arrived late to a Campus Life meeting. He sat down in front of his best friend, who immediately leaned forward and said to him, "Forrest, your head is dripping with blood!" He was completely unaware of it. Apparently, he had fallen somewhere along the way, had come around and then just went on to the meeting.

When he was in Colorado Springs, he would often call and say, "Guess where I am?" Typically he would be at a hospital or clinic emergency room, but always in good spirits.

As I watched Forrest make friends, I saw how careful they were to learn what would happen with him and they were quick to help him. It gave me a lot of peace. Also, my good friend, Harriett Corbin, lived in the Springs. Forrest would go to visit her, and she would take him to church. Harriett prayed for Forrest faithfully.

All of these good things were evidence to me of God's hand on Forrest's life. He finished college in four years and graduated with full cap and gown in 1977. For Forrest, the greatest part of the celebration was that he did not have a seizure on graduation day. He was very frightened that he might have one and pass out during the ceremony, but he made it through. When Forrest returned home from Colorado College, he told us it was the best four years of his life.

Shortly after Forrest came home, he began to have very intense headaches. We took him to see his neurologist, and he called for a surgeon. They performed a CAT scan and determined that surgery was now absolutely necessary.

They told us, "We have to go in to save his life because the tumor is now consuming his brain." Forrest was given only a 50-50 chance of recovery, and right after the surgery, one of the doctors gave him only three to six months to live.

There was no fear in Forrest. He knew what the doctors were saying, and because he was over 21, he had to sign all of his own release papers. The doctors explained everything to him, including that if he did survive he would, most likely, suffer some paralysis, either partial or even full paralysis. In response, Forrest just said, "That's fine. Jesus will take care of me."

Even the night before, when several of his CC friends came to visit him and to pray with him, they came out of his hospital room saying, "We came to encourage Forrest, but he has inspired us."

After the surgery, Forrest did deal with some paralysis on the right side and the seizures persisted, including during the next year, 1978, while we were in England for a Lambeth Conference. This was the gathering of senior members of the Anglican clergy from around the world. All priests were invited in those days, and Chap had really wanted to attend as it was, and still is, held only every 10 years in Canterbury.

Forrest and I tagged along, but because Chap had meetings all day, we stayed with my brother, Cyril, and his wife, Joyce, at their home in Mitcham, Surrey.

One day, we went out to the grocery store. As we finished our shopping, Forrest and Cyril were walking outside while Joyce and I collected the groceries to carry them out. Suddenly, Cyril ran back in, panicked—Forrest had had a seizure in the parking lot.

I was prepared to just let Forrest come around as he usually did, but Cyril and Joyce, who had never seen him have one, insisted we call an ambulance. At the hospital the doctors only had x-ray available to exam Forrest's head, as there weren't many CAT scans in England at the time.

They thought everything appeared to be fine, but they wanted to keep him in the hospital overnight for observation. I called Chap to inform him, and he had everyone at the conference pray.

The next morning the doctors told us, "He seems to be all right and he's maneuvering around well. It doesn't appear he sustained any injury to the head."

So they released Forrest, and Chap came to pick us up and take us back to the conference in Canterbury. But Forrest continued to complain of his head aching so badly that he couldn't sit up for very long periods of time.

The Lambeth Conference was just ending, and we were set to drive down to see my cousins, Jim and Kate Davis, in Wales. We decided we should go ahead with our plan and see a doctor once we got there.

In Wales, the doctor was not sure why Forrest should still be suffering so badly. She wanted him to have a CAT scan, but she told us there was only one in a nearby hospital in Swansea and the waiting list for an exam was about six months, due to the national health care system in England.

Then, she said, "Well, it could be possible to get it done right away if you would bring him in after hours, about 9:00 or 10:00 p.m."

To us, God had made a way. Forrest had the CAT scan that night and the doctors found that he had fractured his skull. There was still nothing that could be done for him. The skull just had to heal and it would be a slow process.

That's what it was like with Forrest from the very start of his seizures. It was anytime, anywhere—and you never knew what to expect.

There was one experience with Forrest I would describe as utterly miraculous. One evening Forrest went outside at the front of the house to watch a beautiful sunset. It was summertime on a Tuesday because Chap had gone to a Kiwanis meeting. Forrest and I were home alone. We had already eaten, and I was getting the dog's supper.

At the front of the house we have a block wall about four to five feet high, at the top of which there is a short fence and a small gate to the grassy yard beyond. I learned later that Forrest had been standing on that wall looking west, of course not inside the fence and gate, when he suddenly had a seizure and fell back on the asphalt driveway below.

Because it had been a while since I'd heard anything from him, I went out to check on him and found him lying there. It was a frightening experience, but again, it was one that drove us to dependence on and to trust in God.

Sometimes with the seizures Forrest would go out and he'd be out for maybe 10, 15, 20 minutes. Then, he would get up and start moving around or moving the furniture. Sometimes, he would try to get undressed. It was very unpredictable.

This time he was out for quite awhile. Shortly after I found him in the driveway, Chap drove up from his meeting. Somehow, we got him up the stairs and into bed in his room. We began immediately to pray for him.

Later, when Forrest began to come around, he complained of severe pain in his abdomen. We continued to pray not necessarily thinking the pain was related to his fall, but possibly from something he ate.

By our bedtime, we decided to take turns being in the room with Forrest to see how he did through the night. So we went back and forth about an hour at a time, and the whole time Forrest continued to be in a lot of pain.

Sometime in the middle of the night, I was back in our room and I began to ask God more earnestly to show us what was wrong with Forrest. It was a mystery to us. I inquired again and again with God, asking first if it was something he ate, or if it could be a tick bite. No clear thought came to me.

Suddenly, an image appeared to me on the ceiling like bright light bulbs spelling the word S-P-L-E-E-N. Nothing had ever happened to me like that before, but I was confident that was the answer.

I went in to Chap and told him the problem was with Forrest's spleen. It was between three and four o'clock in the morning by this time. I put my hands on the area of the spleen and I prayed.

Forrest needed to go to the bathroom, but he was in so much pain he had to literally crawl down the hallway. I told Chap I thought we should call the hospital in Kremmling, about 35 minutes away, because there was no clinic in Granby at the time. The hospital emergency room staff told us to bring him in right away.

There was only one surgeon on duty in the ER and he was already scheduled to go in to another surgery by the time we arrived. He took a look at Forrest and told us he would give him a shot to relax him but that we should get him to a hospital in Denver. He, too, was confident the problem was his spleen.

We rushed home to pack over-night bags and drove down to Denver with Forrest. Again, in those days, there was no ambulance service from the mountain communities.

Once there, they ran more tests confirming it was his spleen and scheduled him for immediate surgery. They asked us, "When do you think he was injured?" We explained he had done it the night before.

The doctor couldn't believe it. He told us that typically when you rupture your spleen you bleed to death very quickly. As he considered Forrest's condition, he was baffled at how the bleeding must have subsided.

I told the doctor we had prayed all night for Forrest, suggesting that perhaps God had stopped the bleeding until we could get him to Denver. We don't really know what happened and how Forrest stayed alive. God knows.

They took Forrest in to surgery and removed his spleen. Even now, all these years later, when I close my eyes, I can see those light bulbs as they appeared on the ceiling of my bedroom. It was so vivid.

In 1988, while Chap and I were traveling to Seattle to be with our son, Allen, for his wedding, and then went on to Los Angeles to be with Holbrook, for the birth of his daughter, we received a call that Forrest had died.

He had been staying at a care facility in Carbondale, Colorado, near to our daughters, Jeanie and Susan. Susan had just been with Forrest for a short visit. When she left him he was going to have his lunch, and while he was eating a carrot he experienced a grand mal seizure and choked. No one was with him at the moment.

From when Forrest was 14 until he died at 33, I look back now and thank the Lord for His help and His presence. Our life with Forrest taught me deep lessons about trusting God—because of his life, my faith grew leaps and bounds.

It was very much life-changing. We never knew what was going to happen from one moment to the next. Once, Forrest had six seizures in one day. We just had to trust the Lord—especially when the seizures were so bad that he'd start turning blue. All I could do was close my eyes and lay my hands on him and pray in the Spirit. Then, when I would hear him take a breath, I would say, "Thank you, Lord, he's still with us."

CHAPTER SEVEN

The Battle of My Life

It began in 1994. I was 73 years old.

I was going in for a hysterectomy because I had been having trouble with what was believed to be a fibroid tumor or benign growth in the uterus. It was on the right side, deep down, and it was becoming quite uncomfortable.

The doctor at our town clinic ran the original test and wanted to do further testing and possibly treatments; we had actually been tracking it for a while. Because of my age, I reasoned that I didn't need to mess with it anymore. Matter-of-factly, I said, "No, I don't want to freeze the fibroid—I want to have a hysterectomy." It seemed the time had come and I knew the action I wanted to take.

The year before, my brother, Cyril, and his wife had come to the States for a visit, and I had planned a large gathering for afternoon tea so my friends could meet them. About 20-30 people were invited.

The day before the tea, my right leg began to ache very badly. I called my physical therapist, and she gave me some small standing positions to use in order to alleviate the pain and still be able to function. I would stand on one leg and put the other on a stool and it would relieve the pressure. I accomplished the tea and it was a lovely visit.

Just a couple of days later, we traveled to Glenwood Springs to visit our daughters, Susan and Jeanie. I felt moved to speak with Jeanie's husband, Mark. He recommended I have a venogram, an x-ray that takes a picture of the blood flow through the veins. The very next day I was able to see the specialist and have the test, but they found nothing. Apparently, they didn't go high enough into the groin. If they had, they would have seen feelers coming down from a large tumor on or near my uterus. That tumor was getting all its blood supply from the vein in my leg, so it was growing rapidly.

Somehow I carried on a bit longer. I didn't think another thing about the leg, and the pain went away for a while. But the next summer, while returning from a driving trip to Albuquerque to visit our son, Holbrook, and his family, we stopped at Susan's. I told her that I was experiencing a lot of pain again, and I had her feel the fibroid that was now quite large and easy to grab hold of. In amazement she turned to me and said, "Mother, you know you don't really look all that great—I think you need to see a doctor." And I said, "I don't really feel all that great. I don't have my usual get-up-and-go."

We decided I should go to the doctor. So when I went home, I scheduled an appointment. That's when the doctor recognized an abnormality, conferred with another doctor, and they recommended further treatment. I felt I had fooled around with the pain long enough, so I put it in mind to have the hysterectomy. In reality, the tumor had been growing all this time—perhaps for years—and we didn't even know exactly what was going on.

In our mountain community at that time, we only had general practitioners, so in order to pursue the hysterectomy I needed to find a gynecologist in Denver. I called my nephew who is a pediatrician and he recommended a physician who had cared for all of his sisters.

I went to see this doctor on a Monday, August 22. He looked at my exam results from Granby, and we scheduled the hysterectomy for the very next day. When I was being wheeled into surgery, I was so thankful to find another Christian there, a woman, who also happened to be the anesthesiologist. She introduced herself to me by name and then said, "This is who I really am…" as she pulled a necklace from inside her uniform that read *Jesus is Lord*. I said to her, "Oh, great. You can be praying for me." And she said, "You can be sure I will be."

When they opened me up in surgery, they discovered it wasn't a fibroid at all. What they found instead was a rather large sarcoma tumor, a rare and fast-growing malignant soft tissue tumor. It had formed and attached to my uterus.

The gynecologist went ahead and tried to remove it. Unfortunately, while doing so, the right main vein, where the blood supply was coming to the tumor from my upper thigh, was also invaded. Pints of blood began to pour out of me, and quite honestly, the doctors thought they were losing me.

The anesthesiologist told me later that when they thought I was dying, she was praying, "No, Lord, she's not going home yet." At one point, the doctor came out and spoke with Chap telling him, "We're losing her. We can't stop the bleeding."

They called another surgeon for help, but they were told because of the bleeding they really needed a vascular surgeon to accomplish this properly.

When they recounted all the events to me later, I really sensed a touch of God and that He had intervened right at that point on my behalf. I was told when they had called Swedish Hospital for the needed specialist—at that very moment—in walked a vascular surgeon, and he responded immediately, heading right to Littleton Hospital where I was still in surgery.

I was in the operating room a total of six or seven hours. The vascular surgeon stopped the bleeding and I stabilized. Due to the original invasion of the vein in my upper leg, there was irreparable tissue and tendon damage. I deal with it even to this day. Blood flow is slow, and whenever I've been sitting a while I need to give the old leg a little time to get going once I first stand up.

Well, the biopsy results came back with the cancer diagnosis. I asked the doctor directly, "Do I have the big 'C'?" Somehow, his affirmative answer did not shake me.

Besides the doctor talking to me, that was the first time I heard an audible voice from God—one of the few times in all my years. Quite clearly

I heard God say, *"I will never leave you nor forsake you. I'm with you all the way."* A wonderful peace came over me—just like the Scriptures describe—a peace that surpasses all understanding. I wasn't panicked. I remember thinking, *"Cancer! Well, the Lord is in control."*

The hemorrhaging during the surgery caused me to be very sick for about two weeks. I stayed several days in the hospital, and then by doctor's orders, we stayed on in Denver with friends. They wanted to be able to check me regularly.

The children weren't able to be with me for very long periods of time. I was going in and out of consciousness due to all the hemorrhaging. Even when I was conscious, I was so very exhausted. They say I remained in critical condition throughout that post-op period.

When I was conscious, I was taking every opportunity to tell people how I saw God working one small miracle after another. I could see God's hand at work in my circumstances. I shared that with nurses and doctors alike. Some of the Christian nurses prayed with me when my white blood count was too low—and when it came up, I would share about the prayer with the doctors.

Finally, the day came when I was allowed to return home. The doctors recommended chemotherapy, but I wasn't ready to make that decision. I resumed a regular routine of running in the deep end at the YMCA pool at Snow Mountain Ranch, focusing mainly on regaining strength in that leg.

I remember thinking, *"Something still isn't right with that leg."* If I put my leg out fully extended, I had to lift it back down with my hands. I didn't have any strength in it.

One day in October, drying off after a swim, I felt something and thought, *"Isn't that odd, there's a little lump there."* It was right where they did the surgery, so I thought it must be scar tissue.

When I saw my physical therapist and mentioned it to her, she said I should contact my doctor and inform him. So the very next day I was back at the doctor who had performed the surgery just a couple of months prior. He did a CAT scan, and when he got the results, he told me, "Betty, you don't have one tumor there—you have six—and the way they have grown, they will consume all your other organs. They'll take over." He went on to inform us that I probably had only three weeks to live.

It was amazing to me how God directed my next steps.

My brother, Bill, was a personal friend of an oncologist considered to be one of the best in Colorado and perhaps even in the United States, Dr. Paul Bunn. Bill wanted me to see him, but when my doctor's office tried to reach Dr. Bunn we were told he was out of town. Not wanting me to wait, they made an appointment for me with another oncologist the following week.

Bill persisted, calling Dr. Bunn at home and learning that he would return home on the weekend. That was a Saturday—and on Monday, I was in his office.

Dr. Bunn took a look at my CAT scan and confirmed the sarcoma tumors. He said, "I'm sorry, I cannot give you any hope. Medically, we cannot treat these tumors—they are very difficult and don't respond to chemotherapy." He also explained that there were too many of them for surgery or radiation.

That was on October 30, 1994, and I was given one month to live. Needless to say, that was a bit of a scare. Somehow, when Dr. Bunn said he had no hope for me, I responded, "Well, I'm a very strong believer." And he said to me, "You'll need every bit of faith to fight what you've got because, medically, it's impossible."

Still, Dr. Bunn decided to try the strongest chemotherapy possible. Initially, I was very against chemotherapy. I had lost a friend recently and her family felt that more than anything else it was the chemo that killed her. But my son, Holbrook, and other family really encouraged me to have it.

I had been through all that consideration right after the hysterectomy and removal of the original tumor. You know it's a difficult process when you're being sort of "courted" for chemotherapy. You feel like it's a selling game—no disrespect to the medical profession—I had truly wonderful doctors. During my post-op several doctors had come to talk to us describing the different treatments, and making their recommendations. For a time, I continued to say, "No." Now, with Dr. Bunn, I saw that it was not wise to delay. I had a sense that God would take care of me.

In between that first appointment with Dr. Bunn and the first chemo, I went to Aspen to see a biochemist, Phyllis Bronson, who was highly regarded by my daughter, Jeanie. I worked very closely with her, taking a high-potency vitamin supplement powder and other products to build me up for the chemo. My family and I felt this was absolutely essential for me.

About a week later, on November 8, we started treatment. I began with a 96-hour continual round of chemo. I can still remember those two black bags hanging near my bed and the nurses replacing them regularly throughout the treatment, which lasted from Monday through Thursday. Then, I returned home.

After that first treatment, I had a blood test at our local clinic and they faxed the results to Denver. When my doctors in Denver saw it they called immediately, telling us: "You've got to bring her down right away." It was night by them and would require a two-hour drive from the mountains into town, so they gave us permission to go back the next morning. Apparently, my white blood count was extremely low.

That evening some of our children were with us in Granby, and a close friend, Carla Craig, had come by to see me. With the low blood count I looked very ill, so Carla said to Susan, "We must prepare ourselves—Betty is dying."

That next morning, as Chap was getting the car ready to go, I lay down on the sofa. I was just so weak. I guess my eyes were closed and my mouth was open. So when Holbrook walked by he said to Bruce, "I think she's gone."

"No, I'm still here," I said.

At the hospital they began giving me blood right away. I ended up needing five pints of blood, and I was kept in isolation from about November 15 until Thanksgiving.

The doctors were working just to bring my white blood count up, and even more than that, they were working to stop the fever that persisted. This was absolutely necessary before I could go back on chemo.

It was so strange, really. Chap and the children could come see me, but they couldn't bring flowers or any outside food—no fruit or vegetables— anything fresh. The hospital wouldn't allow for any potential germs.

By Thanksgiving Day my temperature came down to 99 and Dr. Bunn said, "Send her home." The nurses had all been rooting for me, and I felt it was a miracle.

I could eat, but I wasn't very hungry because the tumors were now pressing on my stomach. They were quite large. I actually looked about six months pregnant. Not being able to attempt any more chemotherapy until I stabilized, it was a time of waiting.

We were aware that there was a great amount of prayer going up for me during all of this diagnosis and surgery and the early days of chemotherapy. That fall, our national church convention was being held in the Midwest and Chap had called to inform them, and the whole convention prayed. People from other churches in the area, and friends from Denver—so many people—were praying for me. Even though I was very ill, the knowledge of these prayers comforted me, and I believe they comforted my family too.

Chap was a very quiet man. He didn't show emotion and would tend to withdraw. The children would call and ask, "How is Mom?" He would say, "Oh, she's fine." So they would press him a bit saying, "Dad, we know she's dying." I knew he didn't know what to do or what to say—he just prayed quietly and trusted God.

By the time we got to Christmas, the family literally thought it might be my last, so they all planned to come together at our home in Granby. Dr. Bunn wasn't sure I would even live until Christmas. I didn't care about my prognosis at that point. It was just wonderful to have everyone around me—all my children and grandchildren. I remember that as one of the most wonderful Christmases.

With January came a return to the hospital because Dr. Bunn wanted to try more chemotherapy. I was receiving the usual regimen of treatment followed by a three-week break. After the second round he cut back the dose—not the hours, just the dosage. I had CAT scans every three months to check the progress. I did six rounds of that—first chemo, then CAT scan, then get the results—and over again.

By the end of the second or third round, I remember being at Dr. Bunn's office for a check-up. He said to Chap and me, "They're shrinking!" He was a very proper man—tall, handsome, white haired, about in his 50s—but I could tell he was very pleased. I said, "Oh, praise the Lord!" And he said, "Yes." This was something he thought would never happen.

That was the turning point. Dr. Bunn said I was a miracle. I went on to complete six rounds of chemo altogether—same dosage, same 96 hours.

I began to not mind the hospital time. I got to know everyone who cared for me there, and it was a joy to talk with each one—to speak about the Lord and His goodness. They had witnessed that something quite profound had brought me through this dark hour.

It was during the sixth round of chemo, with the tumors still shrinking, that Dr. Bunn came to see me with another oncologist with whom he had consulted. They said, "The decision we must make jointly is whether we go on with a seventh round or go back in now and remove these tumors."

The consulting doctor said he didn't believe I would get much more benefit from another round of chemo. He described how hard it had already been on my body, so he recommended we go ahead and schedule surgery. I felt complete trust in their opinion.

We set the surgery for April (this was now 1995), and Dr. Bunn introduced us to Dr. Nathan Perlman, who would be the surgeon. Dr. Bunn was, and is to this day, very specialized. He researches new types of chemo being made available to cancer patients, determines the amounts to be used, and sees patients, but he does not perform surgery.

When Dr. Bunn referred us to Dr. Perlman and described the surgery to us, I remember asking, "How long will the surgery take?" I had some concern because the first surgery had taken almost seven hours.

Dr. Bunn said, "Well, knowing Dr. Perlman, he could be in there for seven hours—or 20!" He assured us that Dr. Perlman was meticulous in surgery—not closing anyone up until he was absolutely sure there was no minute cancer cell left undetected.

Emotionally, as I prepared for this next surgery, I was up and down. At times I felt better and at other times worse. By the time the day of surgery arrived, I was positive and energized. I wanted to get this one accomplished.

We went to Denver the night before. At the hospital early the next morning, I met first with the anesthesiologist. He took me through the usual questions about the medications I was taking. I explained about my thyroid medication, and then I told him I was taking Coumadin. I had been on it since that first surgery because they were trying to cut my blood back after I bled so much. I had not gone off of it.

At that precise moment, while explaining that to the anesthesiologist, Dr. Perlman came in and overheard the conversation about Coumadin. He was shocked. He said, "Nobody told me you were on Coumadin!" Nobody had asked me until now.

He said right there and then we needed to cancel the surgery. If I had gone in without him knowing that, I could have easily bled to death, because Coumadin would have caused my blood to be quite thin. So I went off Coumadin, and we waited about 10 days for my blood to thicken up.

Dr. Perlman was truly a brilliant and meticulous surgeon. The surgery was done, and the next morning when I woke up, I thought all I needed was a cup of water. Just as I asked a nurse for one Dr. Perlman came in again and said, "Prepare her, we're taking her back into surgery." Now, I was shocked.

After this secondary surgery, Dr. Perlman explained to Chap an amazing story. The night after performing the initial surgery on me Dr. Perlman was watching a Denver Nuggets basketball game on television. My name kept coming to his mind. Every time it did he thought to himself, *"No, everything is perfect."*

He rehearsed the surgery over and over. He called the hospital to check on me. He was convinced everything was fine. So, he went off to sleep.

In the night, he woke up and again my name was on his mind. So he came in to the hospital. When he came in and said he was taking me back into surgery, he didn't really know why. He checked all my vitals and everything appeared perfectly fine. Still something nagged at him, and he felt sure he needed to take a further look.

Back in surgery, he double-checked all his work on the left side where he had removed the tumors. Then he checked the right side where he found an artery that was oozing—something that would have become very problematic.

I couldn't have imagined what was wrong. But the meticulous surgeon and an all-knowing God, together they watched over me and brought me through.

Susan used to tease Dr. Perlman saying, "We know why you took Mother back in to surgery—we were praying for you and God kept her on your mind." He would just roll his eyes.

Back in the mountains, in Granby, prayers continued throughout my cancer battle. At Granby Elementary School, where they all knew me as a teacher in years past, one of the teachers organized an "angel shower." I had never seen such a thing.

Every teacher and student was given the opportunity to send me his or her good wishes by sending me an angel. They crafted these angels in the classrooms and then hung them one-by-one on our front door. In the end, 65 angels graced our front entry—all shapes and sizes. One person made an angel garland on a string of lights and hung it across our fireplace mantel. I still wasn't allowed to have visitors because of the effects of the chemo and my reduced immune system. So, it was very lovely to see their expressions of good wishes.

After that surgery, I waited two more months, during which time my hair came back. Soon, I would return for more chemo, and I would lose my hair all over again. I did not finish with chemo until August 1995.

There were rough days after the last surgery. While still in the hospital, I had tubes running in and out through the nose, and I could not eat. I felt very poorly and it seemed quite difficult to get my body moving.

Thankfully, my daughter, Jeanie, was very firm with me. She had always been very athletic—climbing any mountain with her Dad, skiing, yoga—you name it.

Just a few days out of recovery, she began saying to me, "OK, Mum, why don't you hang your legs over the side of the bed."

Because of all the stitches on my stomach, I was quite sore, but Jeanie wouldn't relent. She would keep saying, "I know it hurts, but it will make you feel so much better. Let's just start getting you to move so the blood will get going down to your legs."

So I did those things: First sitting up and dangling my legs, then standing, then walking to the end of the bed, then to the door. She actually had me start doing all these things in the first day out of the recovery room.

When I couldn't go further, I just said, "Enough—I have to lie down," and Jeanie would say, "OK, Mum, that's good."

All my children, and especially Jeanie, were committed to me not becoming an invalid. It was a difficult time, but I had tremendous support.

Our son, Bruce, brought me home to Granby at the end of 10 days in the hospital. I didn't think I could drink or eat anything. We all went to bed, but I put in an awful night with strong pain. Bruce came in and checked on me periodically. At one point, I felt so sick I thought I might throw up. He asked if he should take me to the local clinic or back down to the hospital. At times I thought, *"This is it."* Still, I didn't want to go back.

Bruce called and spoke with the doctor who said it was very important for me to start drinking—he was concerned that I might be dehydrating. So I started forcing myself to eat a little and drink a little, and I didn't have to go back. I began getting stronger.

Through the remainder of 1995 and on through 1996, this was the long road to recovery. After the first three months, I returned for a CAT scan. My hair had started growing back. The surgery had been in April and in July we started more rounds of chemo. Dr. Bunn said this was necessary. My scans came back clear again and again.

So it became a very familiar routine, but something new did happen—a first for me—I went into a kind of depression. I wasn't interested in anything. This was during the chemotherapy in July and August 1995.

I remember one of my nurses really encouraging me to snap out of it. But there were times I felt I was going to pass out and sometimes I just wanted to. Every time I went in for chemo, I would see Dr. Bunn and he would ask how I was feeling. I was honest with him, telling him I didn't feel all that great—not really myself—sort of depressed. He explained to me this was normal for cancer patients.

I saw a specialist. We were considering putting me on an anti-depressant, but I learned quickly that was not the path for me. I tried one prescription, but I learned that I respond quite sensitively to prescription drugs. The first night on that medication, I was back at home and I put in a terrible night. I was hallucinating.

Bruce was still with us, and the next morning I told Bruce and Chap that I wouldn't take any more drugs. I felt I would rather battle the depression than lose my mind, which is what it felt like.

I was headed for a breakthrough in 1996, but there was a deep, dark tunnel of depression, and I would say spiritual oppression, which I had to face first.

Having come to faith in God during the height of the charismatic movement, I was not afraid of the gifts of the Holy Spirit. I knew that God was good and that God's gifts were good. This might be quite a foreign thing for some to consider, but when you are exposed, as I was, to excellent and balanced teaching, and had profound personal experience—there was nothing to fear.

During this phase of my cancer recovery, I needed every bit of the fullness of God to see me through. At times I felt quite strongly I was battling a spirit of death.

In fact, at one point in between chemo treatments, I attended a one-night women's retreat at the home of a good friend. A missionary from Colombia was the speaker and led us in a special time of prayer.

At one point she said, "Let's pray for Betty that her cancer does not come back." I was feeling pretty well at the time. My hair had come in, and I had gotten through that initial bout of depression. Yet other bouts kept reoccurring.

As the women began to pray for me, I collapsed on the floor. I was having a difficult time breathing and remember feeling like there was something around my neck. Another friend helped me up and began speaking in prayer directly to the spirit of death, casting it away from me.

When I got home that night, I was feeling much better. The next day the missionary and her assistant came to visit us and prayed again with Chap and me.

For a period of several months, strange experiences persisted. I could be feeling perfectly normal, and suddenly, I would feel as though I was about to pass out. I would experience panicky episodes of not being able to breathe. Some mornings I didn't want to get out of bed. I thought I was losing my mind—thought it would be easier to just give in and give up. Other times, I could be doing something as simple as sitting down to eat a sandwich for lunch and a wave of bad feelings would come over me.

One particularly frightening encounter happened in the car coming over the Trough Road near Gore Pass, on our way home from our daughter Susan's. I was with Chap and we were listening to tapes of one of our favorite Bible teachers. At one point, in addition to the voice on the tape I heard another voice, quite audible. It said, "I didn't get your body, but I'm going to get your mind." I had never heard that voice before, but I felt sure it was the voice of the enemy of our souls.

That was the most dramatic experience and each one sort of built on the other—over and over again—until one Sunday after church. Susan was visiting, and she and I had come home to begin preparing lunch. Suddenly, I just started to shake. Susan had me sit down on the couch, and we began to pray.

After a while, she said to me, "You have a strong faith, Mother, but you have a lot of cracks." She helped me recognize that I was battling a question of my worth as a person. Since the cancer and the chemo I hadn't really been able to pray, to read the Bible, or to go to church regularly. I felt worthless.

Even though I wasn't aware of it before, my faith was very much based on my ability to do certain things in order to be accepted by God and others— even to be accepted by myself.

Susan ministered to me for about two hours, going through all the Scripture verses I had recorded in a little blue book that I kept with me for encouragement throughout my surgeries and chemotherapy. We read the verses and I clung to their truth.

One particular passage stood out to me and has stayed with me ever since. It is from the New Testament Book of Romans, Chapter 8, verses 38-39, which reads:

> *"For I am convinced that neither death nor life, neither angels nor demons, neither the present nor the future, nor any powers, neither height nor depth, nor anything else in all creation, will be able to separate us from the love of God that is in Christ Jesus our Lord."*

Something broke through that day. It was a dramatic turning point in my life. God's grace was given to me and I was set free. Through the prayer and the Scripture, God delivered me from the torment and I have not returned to any sort of depression since. It was a wonderful testimony to me and to everyone.

The strength and help I experienced made a tremendous impact on me. I knew the episodes were what would be called spiritual battles, and I knew powerfully that my help, my way through to live on in freedom and joy, came only from God.

In just another year, February 1997, I would need to call upon God's help once again. I had returned to the doctor because I started experiencing ex- cruciating pain in my back. Sometimes the pain was so bad—it would go down my sciatic nerve—I could do nothing else but get on the floor and put a pillow over my head and scream right into it. Chap would come and pray for me.

When I saw the doctor, he ordered a CAT scan that showed a tumor on my spine. I was sent to an orthopedic oncologist, and he ordered an MRI. I was headed into one of the most painful experiences I had ever known. I had to lie on my back and not move, which was nearly impossible to bear. The noise of the whole procedure was terrible. At one point I thought, *"Well, they are not going to take me out of here until they get what they need, so I'll just pass out."* That's all I wanted to do.

I was scheduled once again for surgery, and the doctor went in to see what he could remove of the tumor. He discovered he could not touch the tumor because it was too close to my spinal column. However, he removed the tumor's feelers that were getting their blood supply from the sciatic nerve, and that's what was causing the severe pain shooting down my right leg.

The next step was radiation to try to kill the tumor. The schedule this time was five days a week, so I had to stay in Denver once again. Radiation is a shorter treatment than chemotherapy—only a few seconds per session. Still, it was so very painful having to lie on my back. They put on my chart, "She moans and groans." Well, it was either that or I would have screamed out loud, and I didn't want to do that. I have a pretty high level of pain tolerance, but this was truly excruciating.

Again the bright spot in the whole experience was the people—those who cared for me. When I first met the radiologist, he asked me to sign a release form. I asked him what it was for and he said, "Oh, you are just signing your life away."

I said to him, "Actually, I can't do that because I've already given it to Jesus."

He asked me if I knew Jesus, and when I said, "Yes," he responded with a great, "Praise the Lord!" He was a wonderful Christian man and every time I went to see him we would share encouragements. He would usually ask me, "What Scripture have you got for me today?"

Almost another year later in 1998, I returned to Dr. Bunn for a routine CAT scan. He spotted a little something on my colon but felt sure it was probably nothing. He sent us to Dr. Perlman who took a biopsy.

Chap and I were getting ready to leave on a trip to Albuquerque to see Holbrook and his family, and Dr. Bunn gave us clearance to go. Dr. Perlman told us he would call when he got the biopsy results—and he did call, just a few days after we arrived there.

He said, "Good news." I said, "Oh great, it's benign."

"Oh no," he said. "You've got colon cancer and that's much better than what you've been having."

I can laugh about that now, but at the time it was quite alarming. Dr. Bunn was amazed at the diagnosis because apparently very few people get two different types of cancer. He explained to us that once a person gets one type of cancer and then cancer turns up somewhere else, it is typically the same type of cancer. For instance if you get colon cancer and it spreads to your liver it is still technically the colon cancer. The same is true with breast cancer. It was very unusual for me to have gotten a second type of cancer, but there you have it—I did.

Yet another surgery was set for June. This time a wonderful priest from Grand County accompanied Chap and me to Denver. He was a priest and a doctor and he really wanted to be with Chap while I was in surgery. I remember this priest praying with me before I went in to the operating room. He was very comforting.

During the surgery, Dr. Perlman came out to speak with Chap and confirmed the colon cancer. He also asked Chap's permission to remove a large portion of my colon that contained the cancer. Apparently, I had an extra long colon and could easily afford to have it shortened. Afterward, I was so grateful to God because the doctor said I would not need more radiation or chemo.

That particular surgery was not pleasant and recovery was difficult, but I had a lot for which to be thankful. That year Chap and I celebrated our 50th wedding anniversary. The same year marked the end of my battle with cancer.

I still go for annual check ups with Dr. Bunn—and so far, so good.

CHAPTER EIGHT

Time to Say Goodbye?

Right after Chap retired as vicar in 1985, he thought it would be good for us to be away for a while to allow the new young priest to get settled in at St. John's. So we traveled to Europe where we made the most wonderful bicycle tour of the French countryside of the Loire Valley. We biked for six weeks, village to village, with scant personal luggage—only as much as we could put into our saddlebags. Still, I felt we were traveling in style. I had one dress and Chap had one shirt and tie, so we were able to dine properly attired nearly every night. It was a magical trip.

Our life was very happy and carefree in retirement. We traveled quite a lot. We made the bike tour to France and we returned to England and Spain to see relatives. We also traveled often in the United States to see our children and grandchildren.

A typical morning for us began with sharing communion and then reading the Scripture for the day. It was a very special practice for both of us, and it set the course of our days. We both remained very active physically and were always with people.

In the winter months, Chap cross-country skied nearly every morning and many mornings we skied together. In the summer months we often hiked up the mountain above Silver Creek with our Black Labrador, Keely.

Chap enjoyed the sport of rowing and in the spring, summer, and fall he continued to go out on Shadow Mountain Lake just north of Granby, several mornings each week. He also continued to study the Scriptures and presided over services at the St. Colomba Chapel, and he stayed active with the Kiwanis.

I kept up my exercise regimen at the YMCA pool, which I have done for years, and I volunteered at school. I also hosted a prayer breakfast along with Bible studies in our home for local women—something I had done off-and-on since the late 1970s.

In the evenings, Chap usually read to me from his library of classical writings. Then we would have prayer and go off to bed. It was a lovely, easy routine.

Volunteering at Granby Elementary as a reading listener was and is a complete delight to me. I had been a paraprofessional there with the kindergarten class from 1970 to 1982, retiring when I turned 65. A few years later I returned as a volunteer with the first grade—I had to take some time off during my cancer battle—and then resumed volunteering once again before I finished with cancer.

The first-grade teacher I assisted, Ellen Auchincloss, wanted me to share about my cancer with the students so they would understand about the disease and the treatment and not be afraid of it. So after my back surgery, I went to the elementary school taking oranges Chap had given me as treat for the children. I gave them out and we sat in a circle. At one point Ellen even asked me to take off my headscarf to show the children my baldhead from the chemo and radiation. It was great, and I think it really helped the children to see there could be humor along the way.

Chap was always athletic—rowing, skiing, mountain climbing—but there were health concerns over the years. In addition to the sprue, he generally dealt with low blood pressure due to a very slow heartbeat for which he had to take medication, and he had a heart murmur of sorts. So we made regular trips to Denver to monitor things.

In the winter of 2000, we were enjoying a wonderful visit at our house with our granddaughter, Leah. One night, after sitting in the corner with

Chap reading to me while I knitted, we all went to bed but I remember putting in a rough night. Chap had been snoring and then getting up and down—he seemed terribly restless. So I slept in Forrest's old room, next to ours.

The next morning at around 6:00, I heard Chap bundling around, so I went in to check on him and found him lying on the floor near the bed. I tried to speak to him, but I could tell that he couldn't hear me.

I called to Leah for help, and as she came in she said, "Oh, Nana, let's get him on the bed." I knew we could not lift him so I told her we should leave him there. Then we called 911.

When the paramedics arrived they began treating him right away—running an IV, giving him oxygen—the whole thing. Then they put him on a gurney and rushed him down to the town clinic.

Leah and I got dressed and we called some of the children. Then I called some people from church and from the community to pray—and we left for the clinic.

Walking into the clinic lobby was sort of like a dream. Just the day before Chap had cross-country skied in shorts, his usual ski outfit, and now I found myself surrounded by people with Chap in the emergency room. It was 7:00 a.m. on a Saturday. It was amazing, really—there must have been almost a dozen people there with us. Our deacon from St. John's was in ministering to Chap, and others were in the lobby standing around or sitting and praying.

The doctors informed us that they needed to life flight Chap to Denver because he had suffered a stroke. Normally, he would have been taken to St. Anthony's by their policy, but I insisted he go to St. Luke's Presbyterian because his cardiologist was there. After a lot of backwards and forwards about permission to do that, when the helicopter arrived the pilot easily said, "Sure, we'll take him to St. Luke's."

Chap still couldn't talk at this point, but our deacon had anointed him with oil and the life flight took him away.

Leah and I drove home to pack and then made the trip to Denver. All the way down the mountain I remember listening to one of her favorite Christian songs at that time, "Shine, Jesus, Shine." By the time we arrived at St. Luke's, I was feeling quite at peace.

Inside our Episcopal bishop had already arrived. He prayed with me and the children started arriving. The unfortunate thing was that Chap's doctor was away on vacation.

The days ahead were confusing as a series of doctors cared for Chap and informed us about what was happening with him. I remember each of them being thorough, but not all possessed good bedside manners. There were a couple of days when only interns attended him, and we got no real information. It was so difficult—we weren't well prepared with what to expect day to day.

Then a neurologist, who was a friend of the family and who had cared for Forrest, came to the hospital and checked in on us. He was so dear and thoughtful, hugging me. He carefully looked over Chap's chart and took great care to explain his condition.

On Tuesday there was a brief bit of activity when Chap was brought out of Intensive Care. The nurses had him sitting up in bed and they tried feeding him a little, but it was a hard process for him. He seemed somewhat agitated and wanted to get out of bed.

By Wednesday, the doctors told us there was more bleeding on the brain. That same day our son, Bruce, arrived from Vermont where he was coaching his cross-country ski team as they competed in the NCAA Championships. The other children—Holbrook, Susan, Allen and Jeanie—were already there, along with two of our granddaughters, Leah and Hannah, and Chap's sister, Sylvia.

On that Thursday, Allen, Susan and I decided to drive up to the house to get some important papers and more clothes for Chap. We drove up in a snowstorm with Allen driving with one hand as he had recently had an accident almost cutting off his thumb.

We spent the night due to the weather and on Friday morning we received a call from the hospital that they would be moving Chap to hospice later in the day. So, we hurried to get back to pray with him before they moved him, arriving just before 6:00 p.m.

We were all together with Chap in his hospital room and Jeanie said, "Let's pray before hospice comes." We prayed for quite a while. Nobody came for Chap.

I remember I was holding Chap's right hand and Holbrook was holding his left—the hand that was now paralyzed due to the stroke. Suddenly, Chap lifted Holbrook's hand and rubbed his own cheek with it.

At that same moment, I looked up at the clock—it read 7:00 PM—and I thought, *"The hospice people should be coming."* Then I looked back at Chap and he was sitting straight up in the bed. Even though the stroke had paralyzed his whole left side leaving his left eye closed—now both eyes were wide open. He looked up toward the ceiling rather expectantly, and then he was gone.

The presence of God was so strong in that room. I said aloud, "Praise God! Thank you, Jesus!" There were many tears, but it took some in the room a while to realize what just happened. I was so thankful that there was no moving him, no going to hospice. He suffered no hard breathing or death rattles. It was a glorious death.

As a family we stayed around him and prayed. We all felt peace and inner strength from God that was completely amazing, and we were carried through the entire time.

Others were coming in and going out saying their goodbyes to Chap. The hospice staff came and asked if they could do anything for us and they offered consolation.

We waited a little longer until the coroner came in to issue the death certificate and then everyone left, except Holbrook and me. Allen was going back and forth between us and the other family as they prepared to leave the hospital. We stayed for several more hours.

MY BELOVED

Before you were born, you were special to me. I knew you before you were conceived in your mother's womb. With my own hands I fearfully and wonderfully created every detail that makes you unique. I knit together your body, soul and spirit.

I saw you long before you ever existed. I watched every day of your life. So I know you. I know where you have been, where you are, and where you are going.

If only you knew the thoughts I have toward you. Did you know My thoughts for you outnumber the grains of sand on all the beaches of the world? You are the apple of My eye. When trouble approaches, I hide you in the shadow of My wings. I have even engraved you on the palms of My hands.

It is My love for you that makes you precious and honored in My sight. I created you for My glory, and I will never abandon what I have formed and made. My goodness and love will follow you every

cont.

The hardest part for me was actually bringing myself to say "Goodbye." I kept going back over to him because I didn't want to leave him there. I would give another hug and hold his hand. He looked so very peaceful, like he was just sitting up in bed.

Finally, one of the hospice staff told us they were going to take him soon and they encouraged us to say our final goodbyes and leave. So we did, and Holbrook, Allen and I drove to a family member's home in Denver for the night.

What comes to me as I remember Chap's death is the Sarah Brightman/Andrea Bocelli song entitled, "Time to Say Goodbye." Chap and I used to listen to that CD often when we would sit together in the evening, and I loved it. Jeanie had given it to me that Christmas. Often, in the morning after we had prayer and while we were eating— I don't know why it would come into my mind—I would wonder, *"Is it time for us to say goodbye? When will that be?"* Perhaps God was preparing me.

Right after Chap died, one of the teachers I worked with at Granby Elementary told me the school children were very worried about me so I went down to the school to visit them. They gave me wonderful letters they had written and pictures they had drawn of Chap with wings up in Heaven. They knew him because he always came around the school with me.

I took the opportunity to talk with the children about death. I told them how much I missed him and that it was okay to cry. Not being employed at the school, I was also able to tell them a little bit about how God loves and cares for us in our joys and in our sorrows. I told them there was nothing to worry about because Chap *was* up in Heaven with Jesus, just like they had drawn him. They asked questions and I answered them simply and directly. It was all very open and easy.

At Chap's memorial service we played "Time to Say Goodbye"—it seemed very fitting. I had now lost two husbands and a son. Of course I grieved—you do. Yet knowing God

day of your life. So do not fret; I will fulfill My purposes for your life. And always remember... My love endures forever and ever!

Psalms 17:8; 23:6; 100:5; 138:8; 139:13-18; Isaiah 43:4,7; 49:16; Jeremiah 1:5

made all the difference. With Henry, I felt utterly alone—I had no relationship with God and I had to face the world alone with my two young children. With Chap, God was near, assuring me that I would never be alone.

That truth was sealed in my heart and mind just one month after Chap died. I was sitting at our dining room table having my breakfast and looking at Chap's empty chair when I said out loud, "You know, Lord, I do miss him."

I had a little boohoo and then decided to try to get my mind off things by doing my morning Scripture reading. I was using my New International Version Worship Bible and the reading for the day was in the Old Testament Book of Jeremiah, Chapter 1. On the facing page was a letter entitled "My Beloved"—a compilation of several passages written together as a message from God to the reader. Well, it was wonderful and the words seemed to be written just for me. They assured me that God was for me and with me, and that He would fulfill His purpose for me. By the time I got to the end of that reading, the message settled inside me.

I know I grieved the loss of Chap as my husband, but it was different—very much so from the loss of Henry. I hadn't been allowed to grieve with Henry and that was very difficult. I'm sure my English upbringing and the sternness of all that also contributed to the way I experienced that loss. Losing Chap, I felt the Lord come in and begin to fill up those places. I was at peace and I trusted God with the future.

That spring I went for a week to Berkeley, California to visit Chap's sister, Sylvia. She had just finished a major campaign called *Save the Bay*, which she had spearheaded for many years. The occasion was a presentation honoring her dedication and accomplishment. Allen joined us, coming down from his work in Alaska.

When I returned to Granby, I got more involved in my volunteer activities. Because I love gardening, I had been helping out at Cold Springs

Nursery on the edge of town for years. Now, I went nearly every day of the week to deadhead the flowers and visit with the staff and customers.

Later in the summer, Holbrook and his family came for a long visit and we traveled to Jackson Hole, Wyoming. What a lovely time—we drove through Dinosaur Park and around the Grand Tetons. Chap had climbed in many of those places, and Holbrook particularly wanted to see them. Then we did a trip down the Snake River that I remember being rather a rough ride. I also made more local Colorado visits to my daughters—to Susan in Glenwood Springs, and to Jeanie in Carbondale.

By August some of my children came to Granby for my birthday. It was a lovely way to end the summer—and in the fall, I went back to school listening once again to first graders with their reading.

Our dog, Keely, became so much more a part of my life. When Chap was alive she was always around him, and I was usually coming and going. After he died, Keely stayed close to me but sometimes she would look for him—going to his closet and smelling around. She really missed him and she was a great comfort to me.

Between volunteering every day at school and time with family and friends, the first year without Chap went by rather quickly. I also kept up with my routine of swimming and walking, and I snow-shoed quite a bit with Keely. There had also been so many letters and cards to which to respond—it seemed like hundreds. People had been very generous and kind.

I will admit going to church was difficult in the beginning. We shared so much of our lives there. I kept attending church in Granby and continued sitting right in the front pew where Chap and I had always sat. Everybody knew and missed Chap, and in his honor the little St. Colomba Chapel in Winter Park was renamed the Cranmer Memorial Chapel.

At times, I tried purposely to keep things light-hearted at church. Sort of playfully, sitting in that pew where I had listened to Chap give his sermons and where he and I later sat after he retired, I would leave a space for Chap. One Sunday a dear friend, Gene Ackley, came over and sat down right next to me in that space. I loved to tease him, so I quickly said, "Excuse me, but you're sitting on Chap." Well, he jumped up and we had a good laugh together.

It was like that, the grieving, sort of back and forth. It was quiet and serious, and also light-hearted. Not too long after Chap died, another friend told me she thought I had done a good job of getting on without Chap and making a life for myself. I told her, "I have the Lord and that's what makes all the difference."

To this day, I deeply miss Chap. I think of listening with him to "Time to Say Goodbye"—hearing that song takes me right back. The life we shared together was a gift—all the wonderful and active years of raising a family, the demands of ministry, and the challenging times of illness for Chap, Forrest and me.

Losing someone you love is an individual journey—different for everyone. I am sure I could not say to someone, "I know what you're going through." I only know what I went through—but I can pray for them in their loss.

Because of my relationship with God, I could see how even the times when Chap and I had to be separated for long periods—like when he went away to seminary—those times helped to prepare me for when he died. There were many times when I would be missing Chap so intensely and then I'd think, *"Lord, you are here. You care for me."* God may not be there in the physical sense, but in the spiritual and emotional sense, for sure. I really do feel God's presence.

CHAPTER NINE

Arriving at Joy

In the days, weeks and months after Chap's death, the challenge before me was to form a life of purpose. I focused my days around these priorities: God, exercise and diet, and involvement with people.

My involvements were, and are, shaped easily around what I love:

- Volunteering at the local elementary school I like to tell the children, "I'm still in first grade!" I go every day and I take turns with the children who really need encouragement with their reading. I listen to them and we review what they read. Having struggled with dyslexia myself, and knowing that so many children in our schools struggle with various reading challenges— it is a true joy for me to be useful to them and to their teachers and families.

- Helping at Cold Springs Nursery is just a wonderful activity for me. I absolutely love gardening. I do plenty of it at home, but at the nursery I get to be close to people and share life with them. Some of them are like extended family to me. I can't imagine not being there, pottering around, caring for plants and people.

- Attending a variety of Bible studies, I like to be ecumenical. I host two studies in my home for Presbyterian and Evangelical women and then attend a study at my Episcopal church and one at another local church. Rounding out my week, I participate with two community groups, one at someone else's home and one in a local coffee shop.

LESSONS OF THE HEART

Healing of Memories —

"Lord, please reveal the things that I need to forgive."

That simple prayer has become a way of life with me. I first learned to do this in teaching sessions with an Episcopalian Bible teacher. She led us through and taught us about the practice of praying for the healing of our memories.

After growing up in England, where people are taught that it is not okay to confront difficult feelings and hurts, this practice was a revelation to me. No longer did I have to stuff the hurts down inside myself.

As I learned to pray this way, I went all the way back to the earliest hurts I could remember. It was like a thorough cleansing. The teacher led us through year-by-year, month-by-month. I prayed, and the Holy Spirit was the One who brought things up. I learned that a lack of forgiveness is a bitter root in our souls that will eat us up, and God

cont.

- Sharing hospitality in my home—especially at teatime is irresistible to me. It's a tradition that I love. I host large and small teas, and low and high teas. Sometimes adults are invited and sometimes children. There are regulars and one-time visitors from foreign lands. The fine china and silver come out and the tablecloth is spread. Over the courses of English Tea, we share life.

How did I arrive at joy? It came to *me*—one step at a time, and sometimes, when I wasn't looking. God faithfully drew me to Himself and gave me a life of meaning.

JOY is not the absence of suffering but the presence of God.

That's a quote from Andrew Murray that I first came across in the 1970s or '80s. My friend, Carla Craig, shared it with me in a card. We worked together at Granby Elementary when I was a paraprofessional with her kindergarten class.

I've kept the card on a shelf in my kitchen ever since.

As I've walked the pathway of my life, I have found Murray's statement to be absolutely true. There is suffering in this world and it touches each of us, but that does not mean that God is not with us. This is something to think about. With the sternness of my upbringing, and the horrors of war up close, I certainly didn't start there. I couldn't imagine that God was good—how could He allow all those terrible things?

As I risked surrendering my life to God, He began to show me how much He loves me and how good He is. He healed my hurts and gave me strength to face all the challenges life brought my way. There is no denying that God brought me peace beyond understanding and joy that overflows.

People tell me I have an amazing faith and I tell them I have an amazing God.

revealed to me those things for which I needed to forgive people. There was no condemnation. It was such a completely freeing thing.

Now, nearly every day, I ask God to show me people I need to forgive. I have come to think, "Why should I carry any of that around?" Today, I can honestly say that I don't feel anything against anyone. It's a very easy way to live.

Memorizing and Praying Scripture —

Being in teaching and fellowship times with Corrie ten Boom made a dramatic impact on me with regard to memorizing and praying Scripture. She would pray God's Word over any situation. It really spoke to me.

I see the practice as giving back to God what He has given to us—it affirms His word. From the beginning of my spiritual walk with God, I began praying this way. It also helped me to commit passages of Scripture to memory. I didn't really work at it or drill myself or say, "I must do this."

cont.

The first time I ever did work intentionally on memorization was when I was training for the "Run for Fun!" in Grand County in the 1970s. I entered the race and began running and memorizing Scripture over a six-week period. Because I had a concentrated time like that, I decided to commit to memory Chapter 17 of the New Testament Gospel of St. John.

Sometimes I carried a couple of verses with me on a small piece of paper and sometimes I just had the verse in my mind. I would repeat it the whole time I was running. I didn't have to run for speed, just for distance, so it was a bit more relaxed. The words of those passages became very active and real.

Even today when I read those verses, they are very familiar. Some of them come right back to me completely. I believe the Lord allows us to recall the verses He wants us to have in our heart and not just in our mind. I don't use those verses in John all the time, but I do have them in my heart.

One particular verse still amazes me over and over again. It is found in the Gospel of John, Chapter 17, verse 22. Jesus is talking to God the Father about us, His people on Earth, and suddenly he says, "I have given them the glory that you gave me, that they may be one as we are one."

Reading that, I stopped and thought, "That's incredible! Father, this tells me that I'm the same as Jesus is to you. How can that be?" I have delighted in that understanding ever since I memorized the passage. That's how I know God's word is living—it is not just black-and-white print on white paper. It's God speaking.

There is one prayer Chap and I often prayed over our children from the New Testament Book of Philippians, Chapter 1, verse 6. It says, "He who began a good work in you will carry it on to completion..." and we prayed that for our children, entrusting God to take care of them throughout their lives. We did that long after they were grown and out of our home.

cont.

cont.

Also, when I battled cancer, I experienced how God brings His word back to you when you need it. I didn't have the strength to thumb through the Bible to find verses, so I kept the little blue book and wrote my favorite verses in there—I especially put in verses about healing. I drew on the strength of God's word from that little book. I just looked at them and said, "Oh, yes, I know."

Practicing God's Presence —

Many years back I read a small book by Brother Lawrence called Practicing the Presence of God. I loved the message of his book and I began to practice his method. I learned that I don't have to be on my knees or even in a quiet attitude in order to pray and be in God's presence.

Brother Lawrence tells that he often had chores to do in the kitchen and could not go to the chapel to pray. He said to God, "If I can't go to the chapel, I know you are still here with me while I do the dishes." So, he prayed all the time while he did his work.

By his writing, I realized that I could enter into God's presence wherever I am and whatever I'm doing because God is always with me. I loved that and began to practice it.

I believe God does desire those special times of worship and prayer on Sunday mornings—that's a whole different thing. But in the day to day, like this morning, when I walked outside—I was in simple communion with God. It was so gorgeous and the sun was just breaking through on the mountains—just two small spots of light—and immediately the words came out from my mouth, "Glory to God in the highest!" "Praise God from whom all blessings flow!" "How lovely on the mountains are the feet of You, Lord!" To me, that's being in His presence, and I can express it.

Practicing the presence of God has become a way of life with me. I talk to God all the time and just pray. Really, I don't know the difference between praying and talking with God. I do it when I'm in the pool exercising, or when I'm walking, or even when I'm gardening.

cont.

10137308R00090

Made in the USA
Charleston, SC
10 November 2011

PRAISE FOR ERIN NICHOLAS

"Sexy and fun!"

—Susan Andersen, *New York Times* bestselling
Playing Dirty, on *Anything You Want*

"Erin Nicholas always delivers swoonworthy heroes, heroines that you root for, laugh-out-loud moments, a colorful cast of family and friends, and a heartwarming happily ever after."

—Melanie Shawn, *New York Times* bestselling author

"Erin Nicholas always delivers a good time guaranteed! I can't wait to read more."

—Candis Terry, bestselling author of the Sweet, Texas series

"Heroines I love and heroes I still shamelessly want to steal from them. Erin Nicholas romances are fantasy fodder."

—Violet Duke, *New York Times* bestselling author

"A brand-new Erin Nicholas book means I won't be sleeping until I'm finished. Guaranteed."

—Cari Quinn, *USA Today* bestselling author

"Reading an Erin Nicholas book is the next best thing to falling in love."

—Jennifer Bernard, *USA Today* bestselling author

"Nicholas is adept at creating two enthralling characters hampered by their pasts yet driven by passion, and she infuses her romance with electrifying sex that will have readers who enjoy the sexually explicit seeking out more from this author."

—*Library Journal*, starred review of *Hotblooded*

"They say all good things come in threes, so it's safe to say that this is Nicholas's best addition to the Billionaire Bargains series. She has her details of the Big Easy down to a tee, and her latest super-hot novel will have you craving some ice cream and alligator fritters. This is a romance that will be etched in your mind for quite some time. The cuisine and all-too-dirty scenes are enough to satisfy, but the author doesn't stop there. This novel may also give you the inkling to visit the local sex store—incognito of course. It's up to you."

—*Romantic Times Book Reviews* on *All That Matters*,
TOP PICK, 4.5 stars

"This smashing debut to the new series dubbed Sapphire Falls is a cozy romance that will have readers believing that they'd stepped into the small Nebraska town and settled in for a while. This well thought out story contains likable characters who grow on you right away, and their tales will make you smile and want to devour the book in one sitting. Four stars."

—*Romantic Times Book Reviews* on *Getting Out of Hand*

"The follow-up to the debut of the hot new series Sapphire Falls will wow readers with its small-town charm and big romance. This story teaches us that everything does happen for a reason and true love can be found even where one least expects it. The characters are strong and animated. It's a complete joy and highly entertaining to watch the plot unfold. Paced perfectly, a few hidden surprises will keep bookworms up past their bedtime finishing this satisfying tale."

—*Romantic Times Book Reviews* on *Getting Worked Up*, 4 stars